Dobby & Louie

A rescue dog and a puppy. Those first two years.

D1564877

Dobby & Louie

Elivia Savadier

elivia

so that's what you're feeling?

ISBN: 0-9973219-0-3

ISBN-13: 978-0-9973219-0-6

Library of Congress Control Number. 2016903945

Elivia; so that's what you're feeling? 2016.

First Edition.

BookLocker.com, Inc., Bradenton, Florida.

Printed in the United States of America on acid-free paper

For Gerry who started it all.

My family who welcome the dogs that enter our lives.

My friends from Last Hope Rescue who have stories of their own.

YOU **ATE**
MY COLLAR.

YOU ATE **MY** COLLAR
RIGHT OFF **MY** NECK.

YOU ALSO JUMPED ON TOP
OF THE GRANDE PIANO,
WHERE YOU DESTROYED
SEVERAL AFRICAN DOLLS
AND SOME BASKETS.

AND You dragged a garden rake
into the living room.
What's wrong with you?

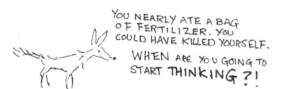

YOU NEARLY ATE A BAG
OF FERTILIZER. YOU
COULD HAVE KILLED YOURSELF.

WHEN ARE YOU GOING TO
START **THINKING**?!

WHAT'S
"THINKING"?

1

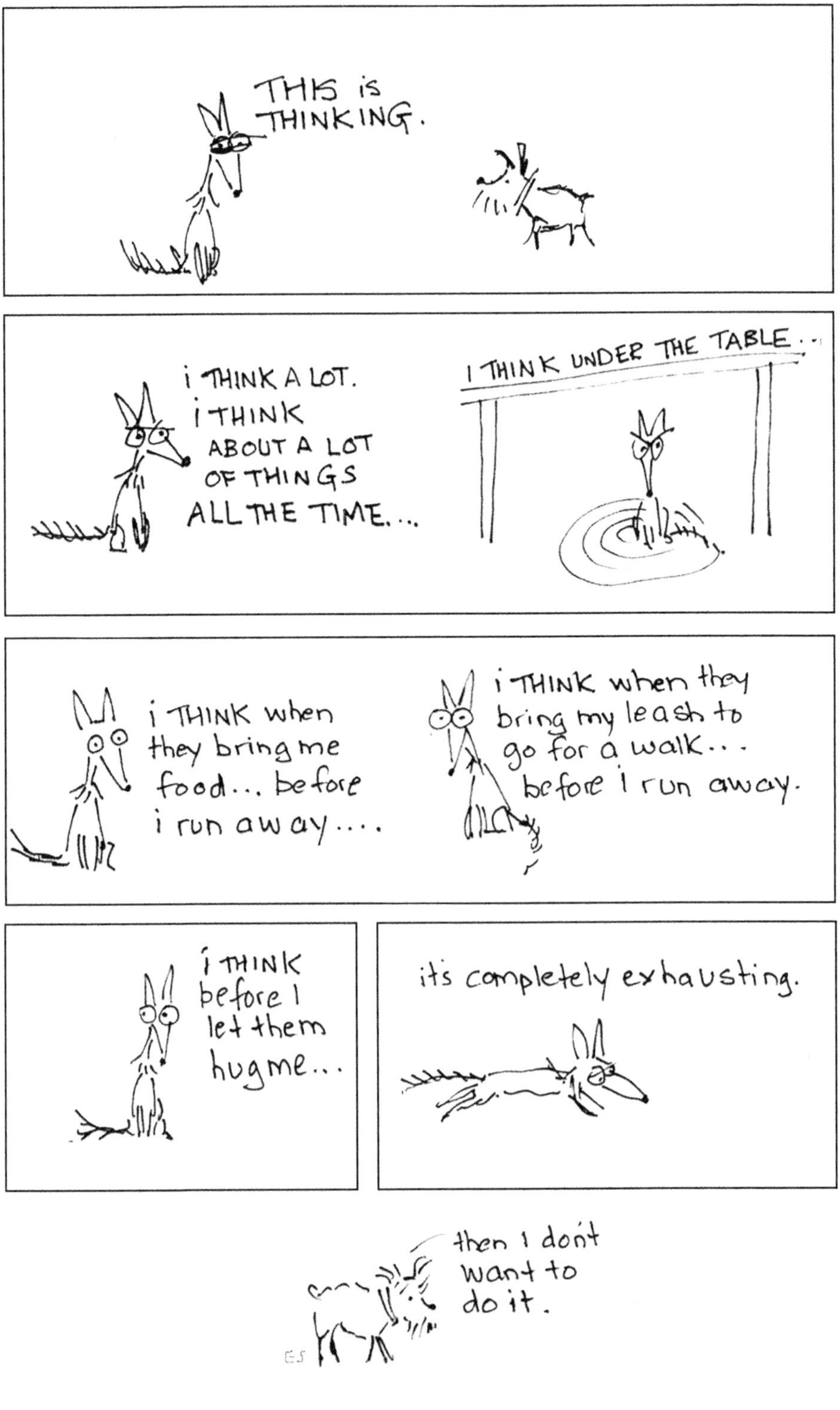
THIS is THINKING.
i THINK A LOT. i THINK ABOUT A LOT OF THINGS ALL THE TIME...
I THINK UNDER THE TABLE...
i THINK when they bring me food... before i run away....
i THINK when they bring my leash to go for a walk... before i run away.
i THINK before I let them hug me...
it's completely exhausting.
then I don't want to do it.
E.S

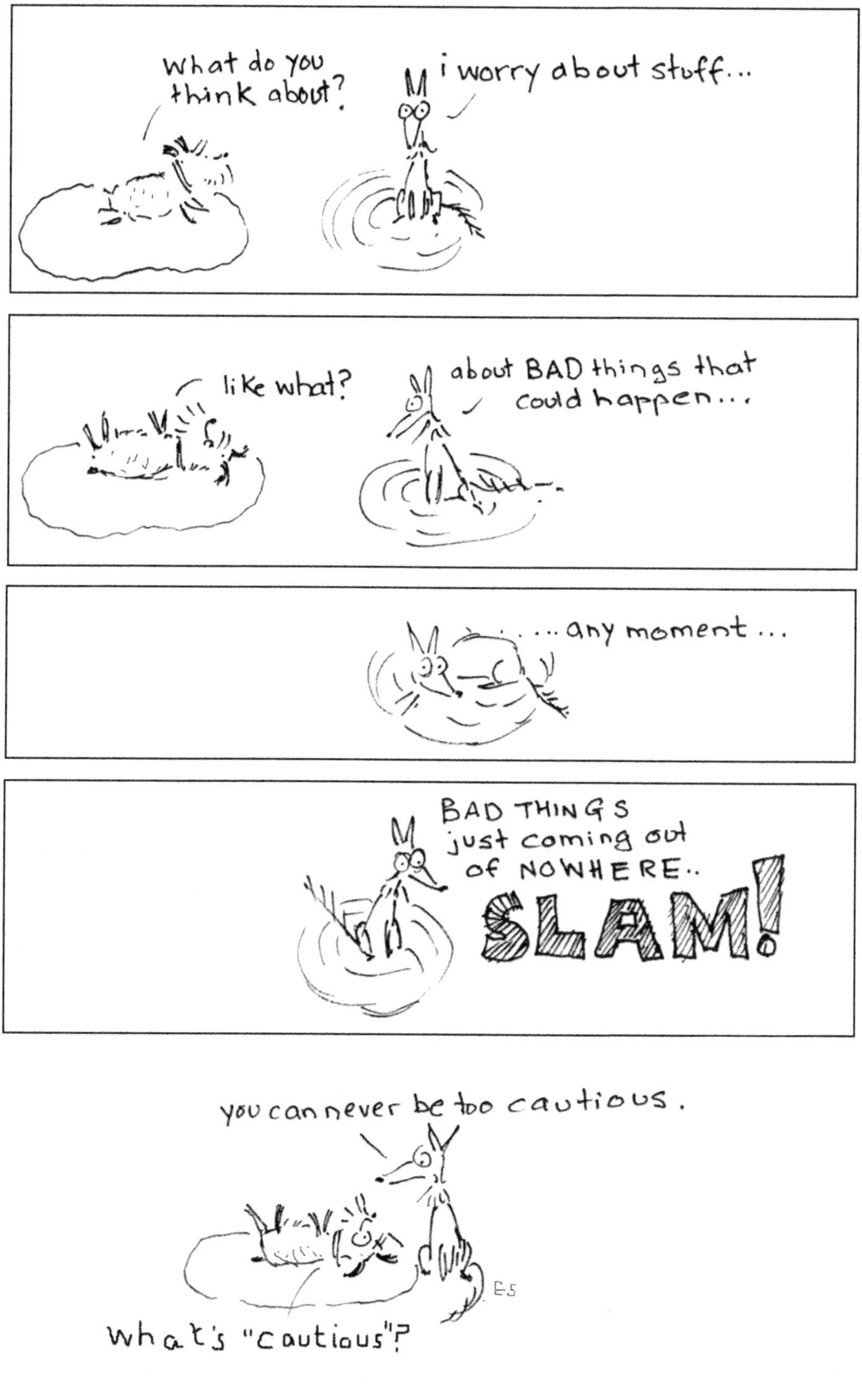
what do you think about?
i worry about stuff...
like what?
about BAD things that could happen...
....any moment...
BAD THINGS just coming out of NOWHERE..
SLAM!
you can never be too cautious.
what's "cautious"?
E.S

How will we know when I'm a big boy, Dobby?

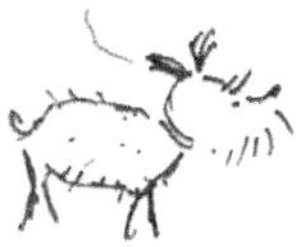

• You won't hide. socks. • You won't chew through carpets. • You won't destroy ornaments. • You won't drag garden rakes inside. • You won't eat fertilizer. • You won't eat their shoes. • After you have eaten their shoes you will not place them on their pillows. • You will not hide your chew bones under their sheets. • You won't poop inside. • You won't steal their tooth- paste. • You won't destroy toilet rolls. • You won't chew through my collar. • You won't drag brooms around the house • You won't hide scrubbing brushes. • You won't.....

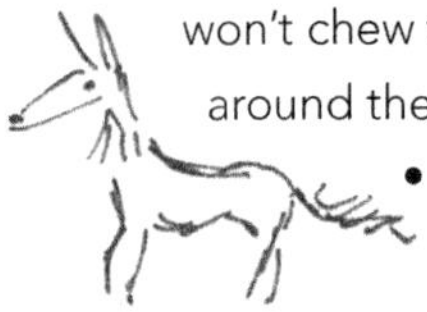

but what else **is** there?

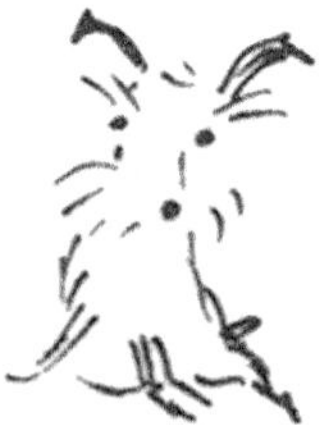

ES

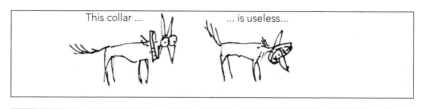

This collar ...
... is useless...

It keeps SLIPPING
... right off my neck.

That's because it ISN'T my collar.

It's Louie's collar.
Because Louie ATE my collar.

LOOK!!
He's half chewed through this one too.

It's hanging by a thread.
He's like an annoying moth ...

EATING ALL MY CLOTHING.
flutter flutter

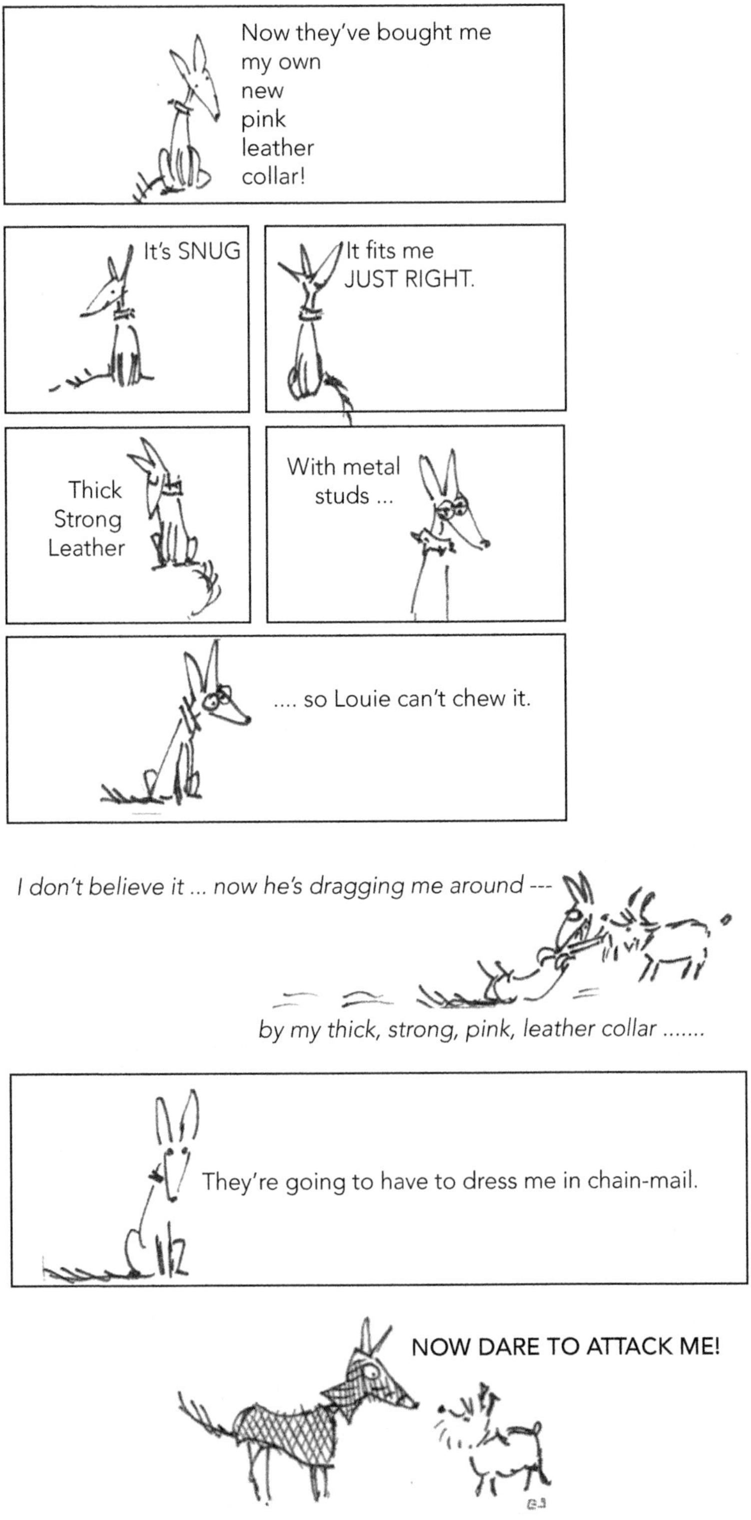
Now they've bought me my own new pink leather collar!
It's SNUG
It fits me JUST RIGHT.
Thick Strong Leather
With metal studs ...
.... so Louie can't chew it.
I don't believe it ... now he's dragging me around ---
by my thick, strong, pink, leather collar ....
They're going to have to dress me in chain-mail.
NOW DARE TO ATTACK ME!

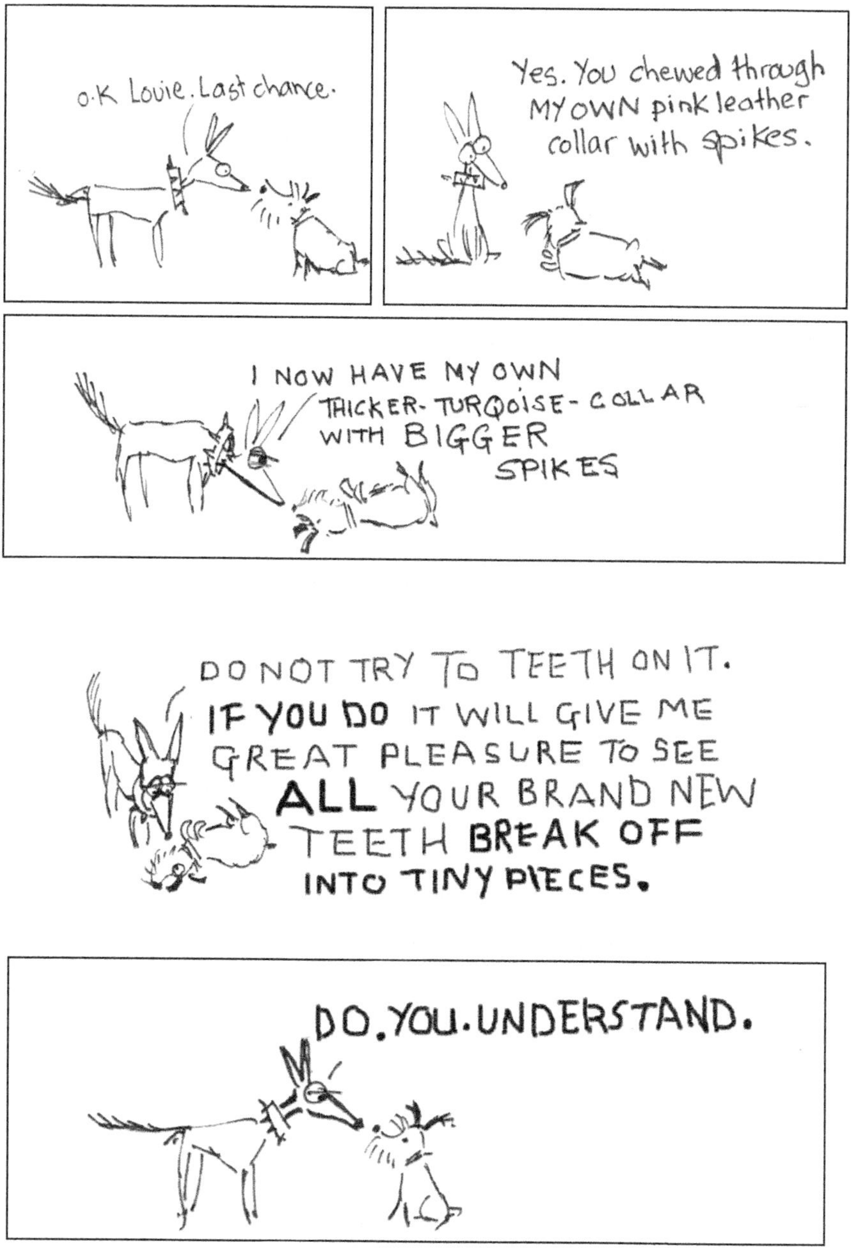
o.K Louie. Last chance.
Yes. You chewed through MY OWN pink leather collar with spikes.
I NOW HAVE MY OWN THICKER-TURQOISE-COLLAR WITH BIGGER SPIKES
DO NOT TRY TO TEETH ON IT. IF YOU DO IT WILL GIVE ME GREAT PLEASURE TO SEE ALL YOUR BRAND NEW TEETH BREAK OFF INTO TINY PIECES.
DO.YOU.UNDERSTAND.

I hope I understand....

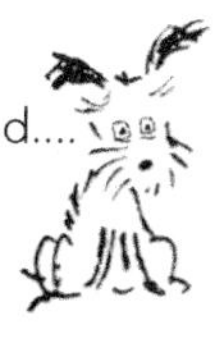

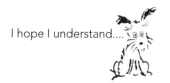

ES

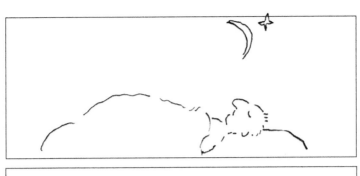

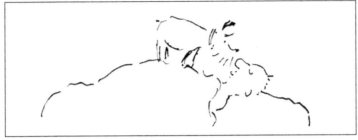

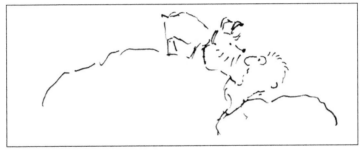

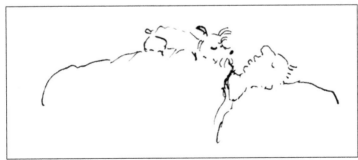

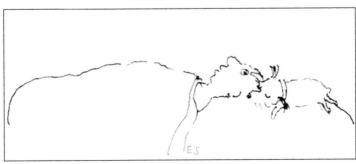

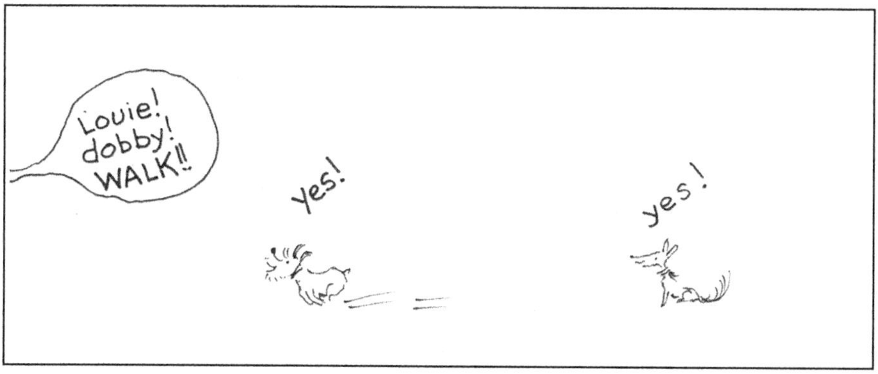
Louie! dobby! WALK!!
yes!
yes!

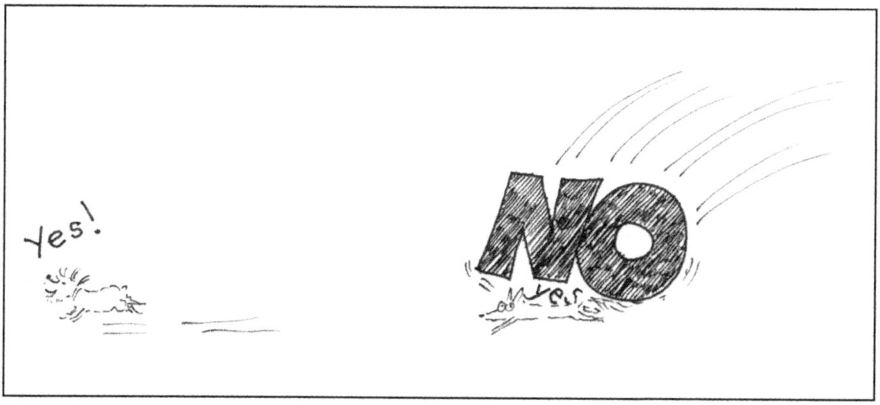
Yes!
NO
yes

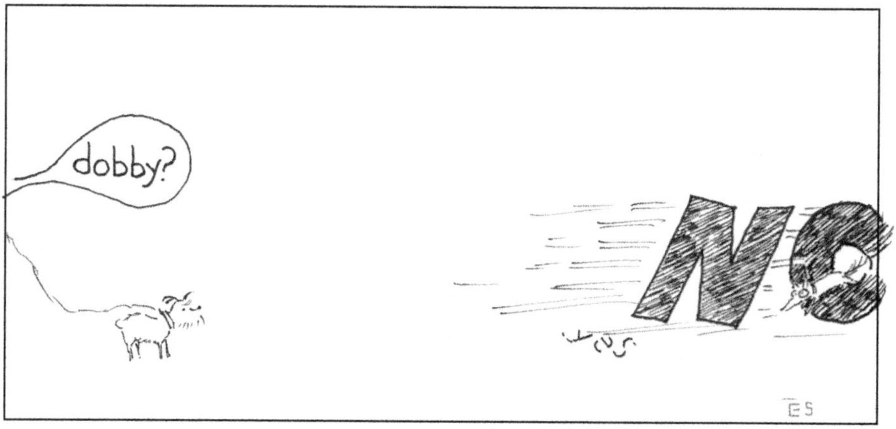
dobby?
NO
ES

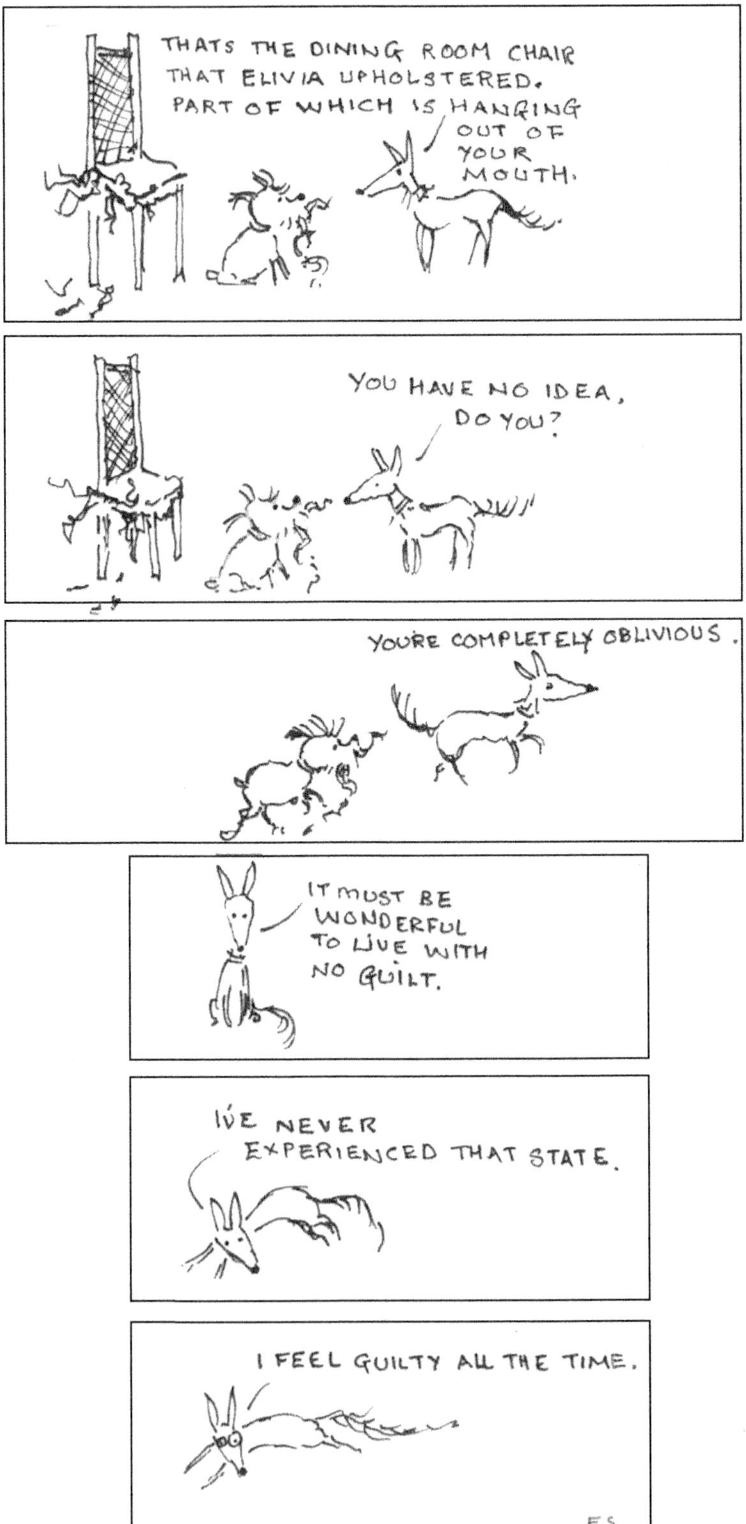
THATS THE DINING ROOM CHAIR THAT ELIVIA UPHOLSTERED. PART OF WHICH IS HANGING OUT OF YOUR MOUTH.
YOU HAVE NO IDEA, DO YOU?
YOU'RE COMPLETELY OBLIVIOUS.
IT MUST BE WONDERFUL TO LIVE WITH NO GUILT.
I'VE NEVER EXPERIENCED THAT STATE.
I FEEL GUILTY ALL THE TIME.
ES

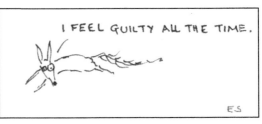

Louie's rampage continues.....

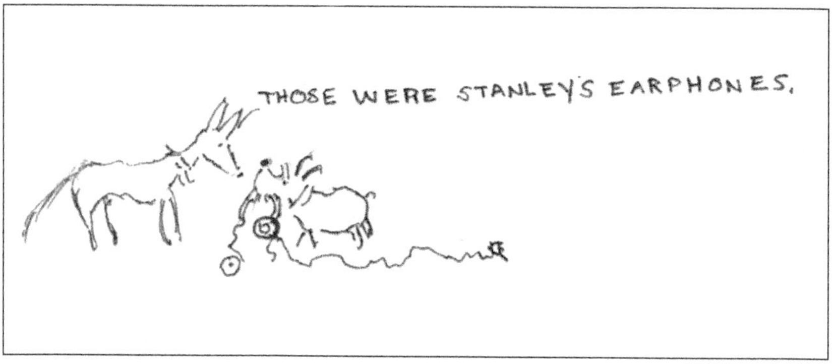
THOSE WERE STANLEY'S EARPHONES.

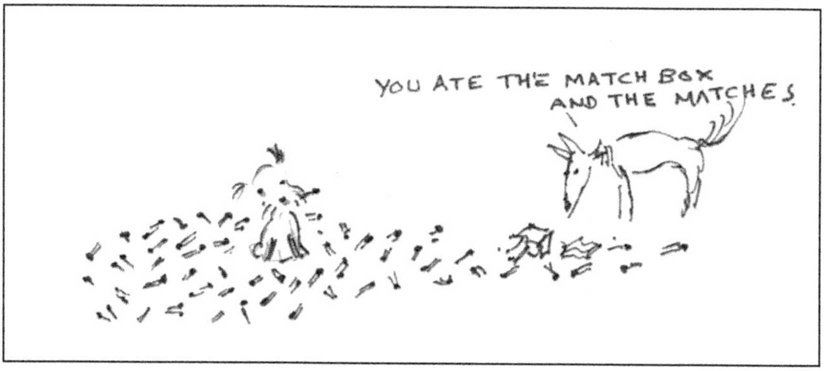
YOU ATE THE MATCH BOX
AND THE MATCHES

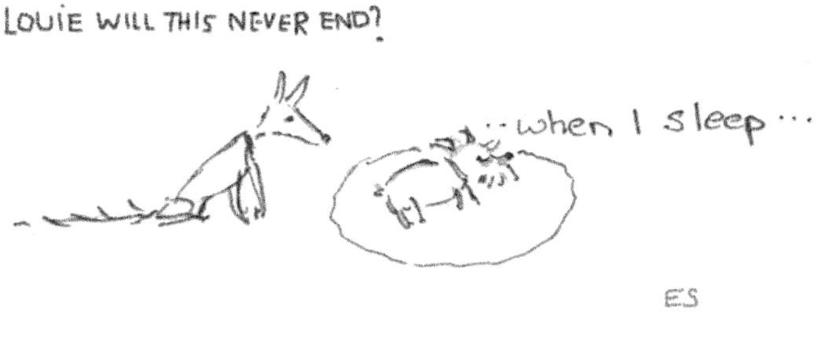
LOUIE WILL THIS NEVER END?
...when I sleep...
ES

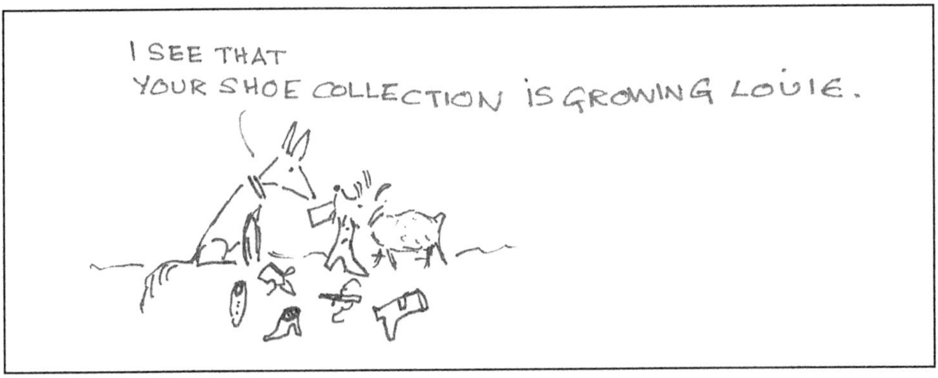
I SEE THAT
YOUR SHOE COLLECTION IS GROWING LOUIE.

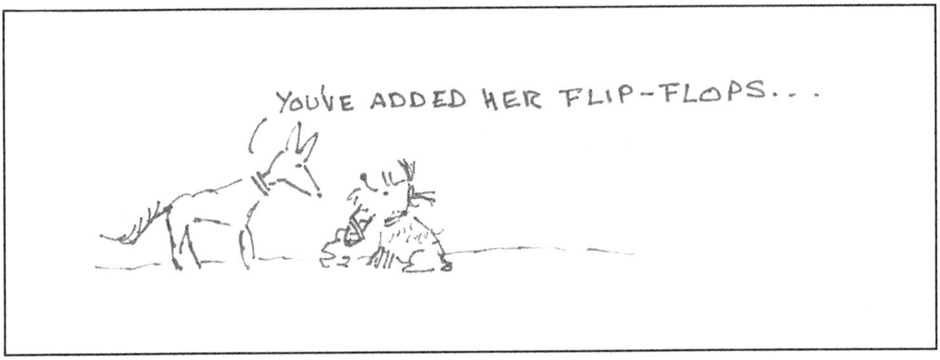
YOU'VE ADDED HER FLIP-FLOPS...

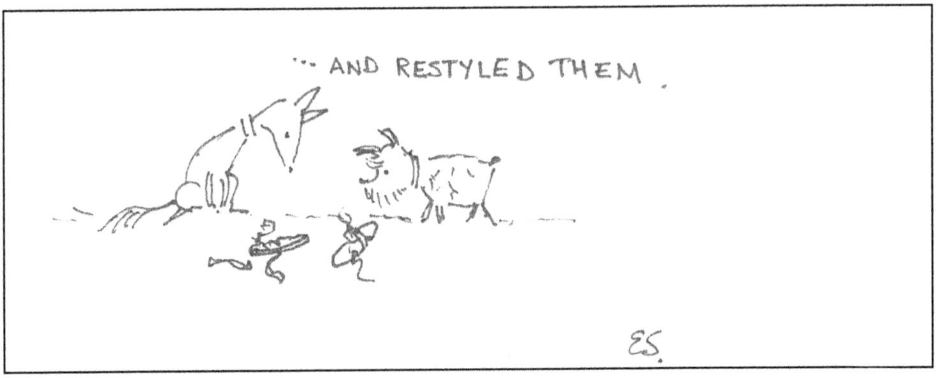
... AND RESTYLED THEM.
ES.

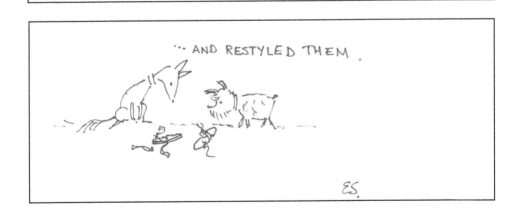

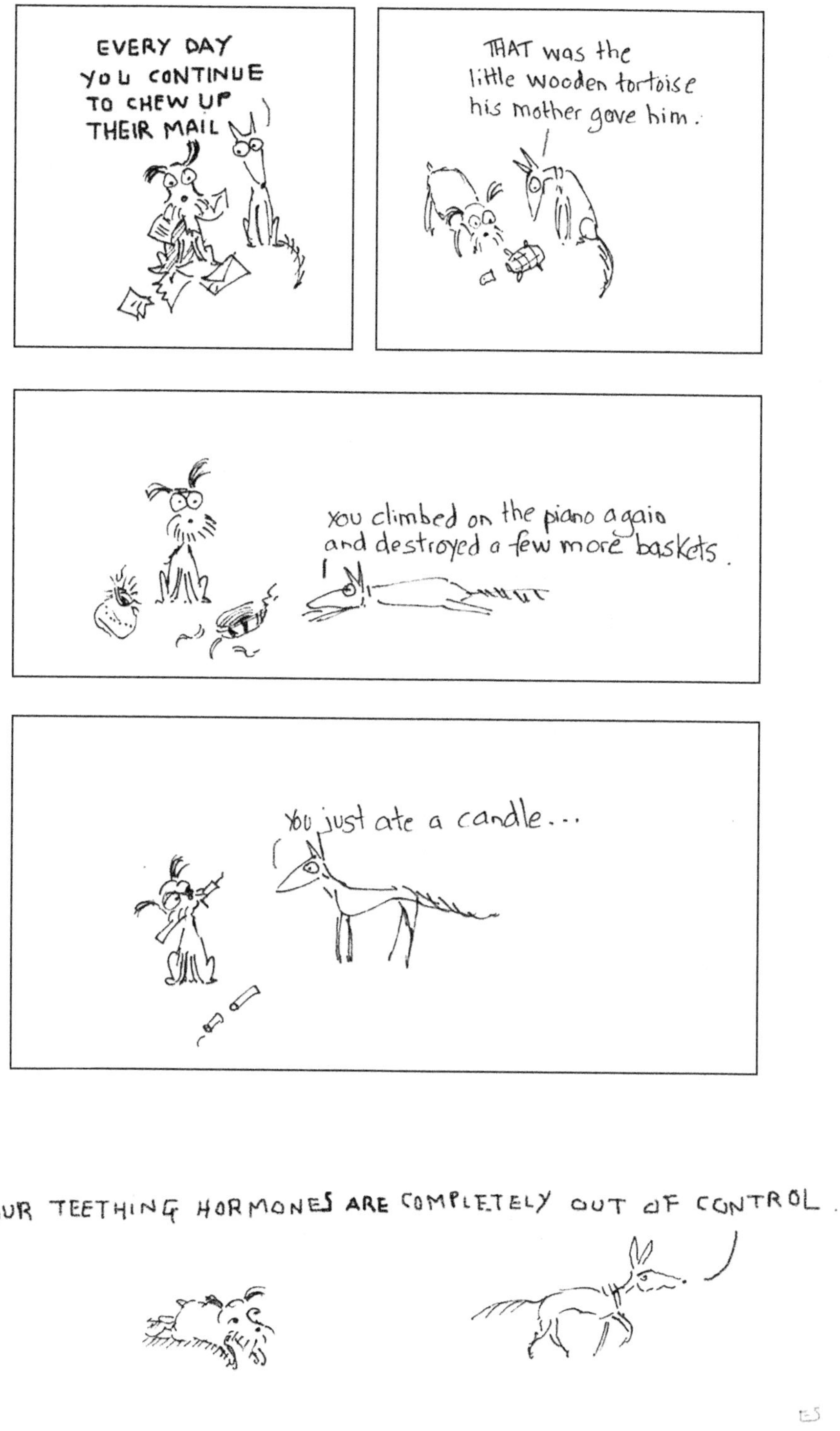
EVERY DAY YOU CONTINUE TO CHEW UP THEIR MAIL
THAT was the little wooden tortoise his mother gave him.
you climbed on the piano again and destroyed a few more baskets.
You just ate a candle...
YOUR TEETHING HORMONES ARE COMPLETELY OUT OF CONTROL.
ES

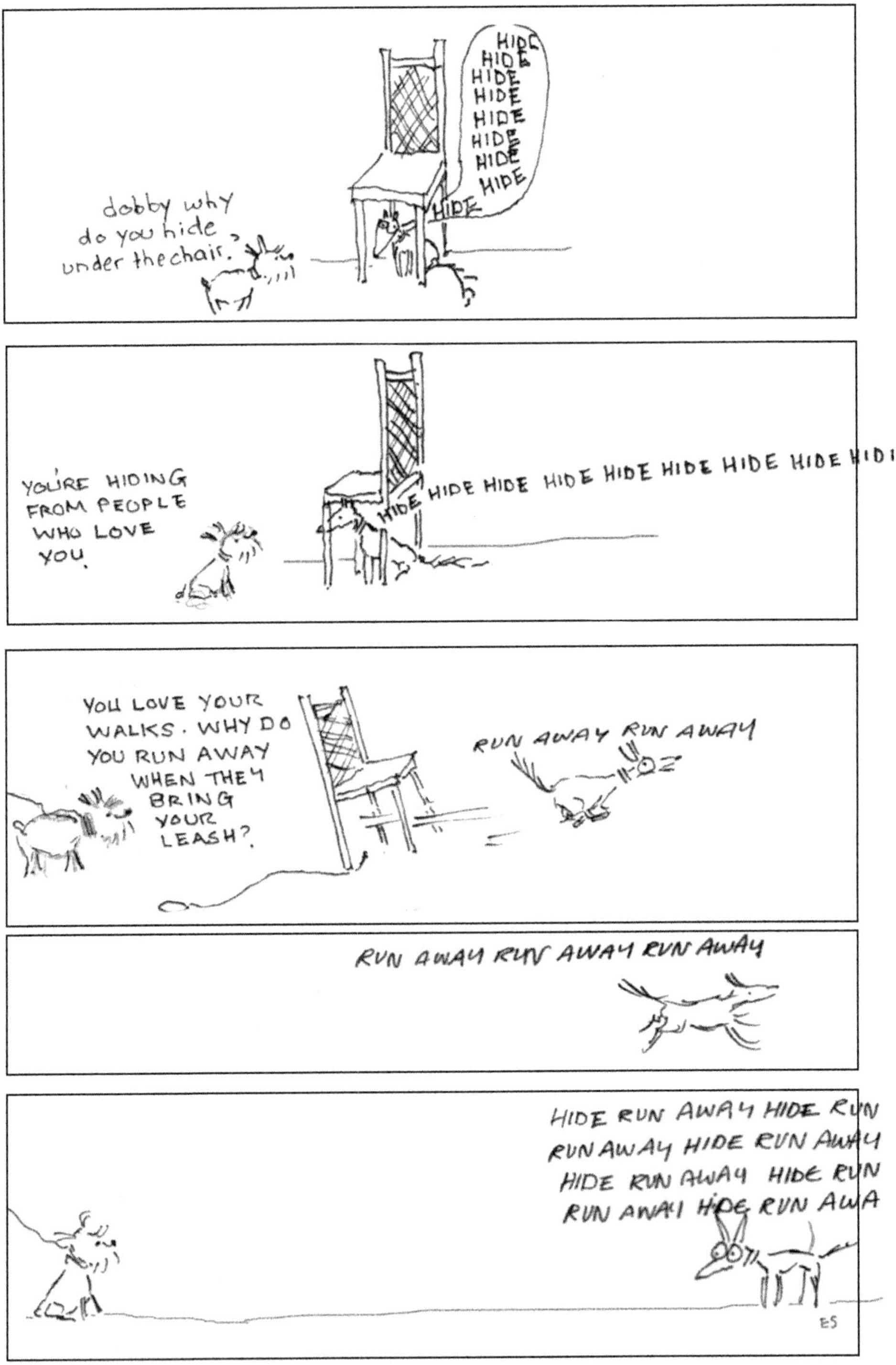
HIDE
HIDE
HIDE
HIDE
HIDE
HIDE
HIDE
HIDE
HIDE
dobby why do you hide under the chair.
YOU'RE HIDING FROM PEOPLE WHO LOVE YOU.
HIDE HIDE HIDE HIDE HIDE HIDE HIDE HIDE HIDI
YOU LOVE YOUR WALKS. WHY DO YOU RUN AWAY WHEN THEY BRING YOUR LEASH?
RUN AWAY RUN AWAY
RUN AWAY RUN AWAY RUN AWAY
HIDE RUN AWAY HIDE RUN
RUN AWAY HIDE RUN AWAY
HIDE RUN AWAY HIDE RUN
RUN AWAY HIDE RUN AWA
ES

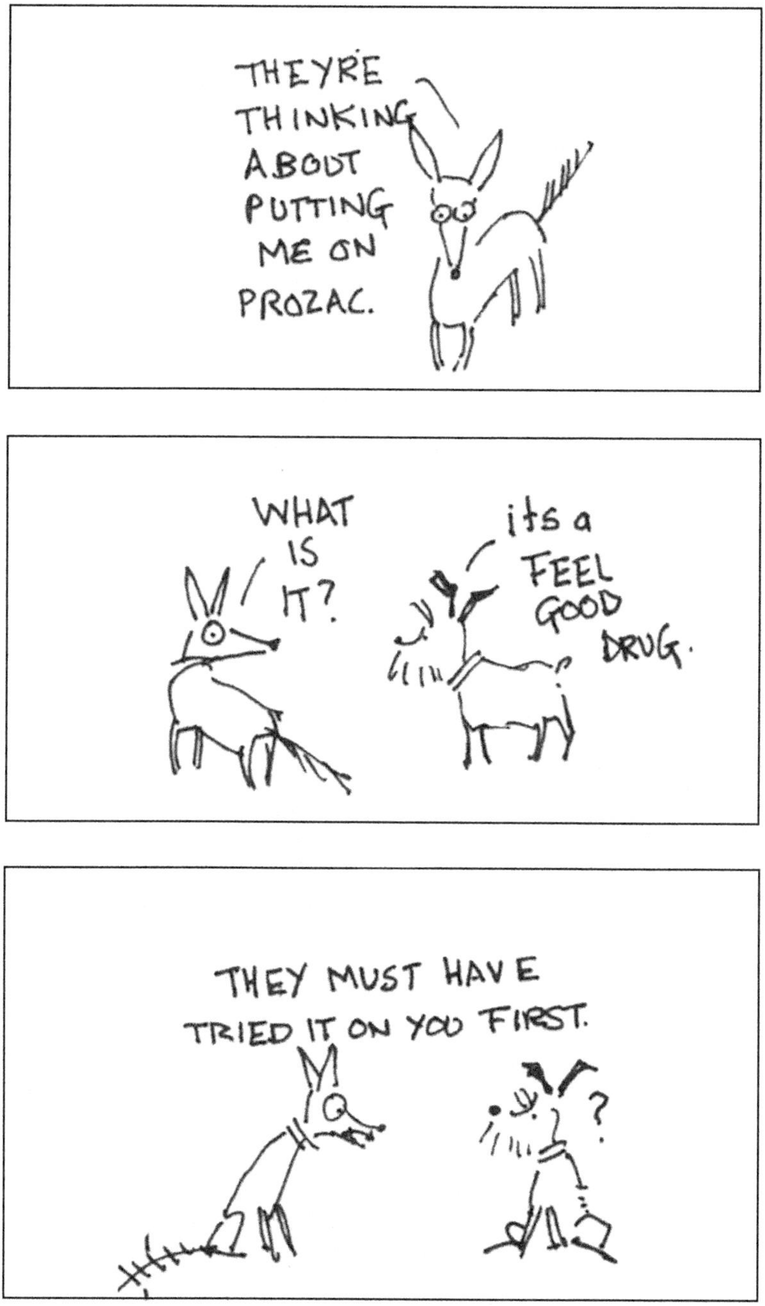
THEY'RE THINKING ABOUT PUTTING ME ON PROZAC.
WHAT IS IT?
its a FEEL GOOD DRUG.
THEY MUST HAVE TRIED IT ON YOU FIRST.
?

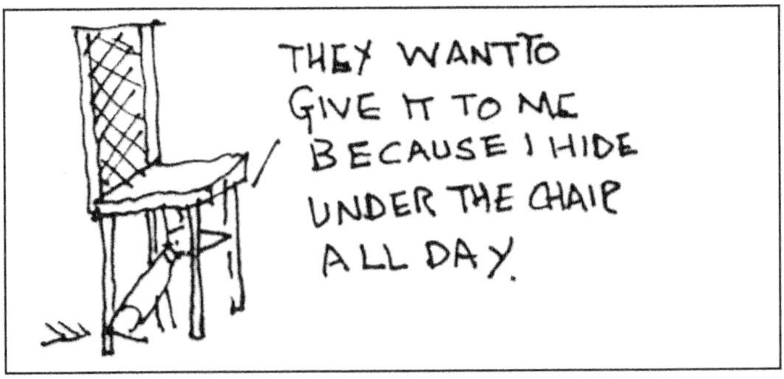
THEY WANT TO GIVE IT TO ME BECAUSE I HIDE UNDER THE CHAIR ALL DAY.

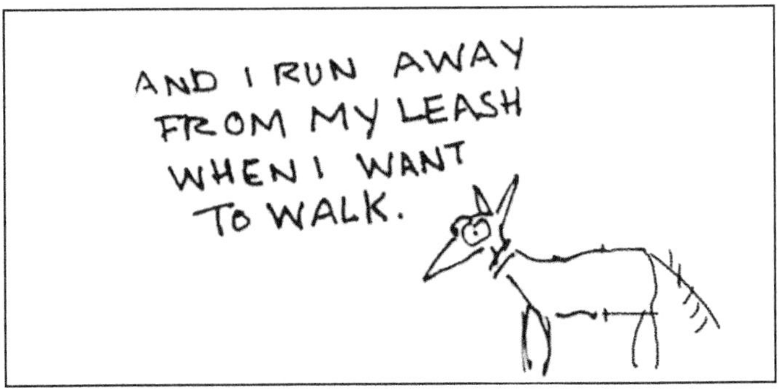
AND I RUN AWAY FROM MY LEASH WHEN I WANT TO WALK.

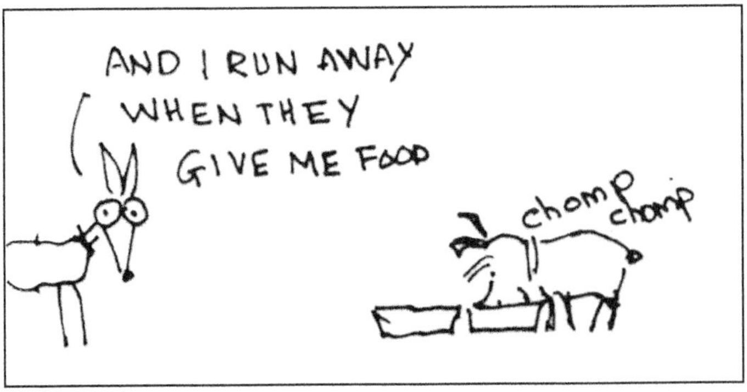
AND I RUN AWAY WHEN THEY GIVE ME FOOD
chomp chomp

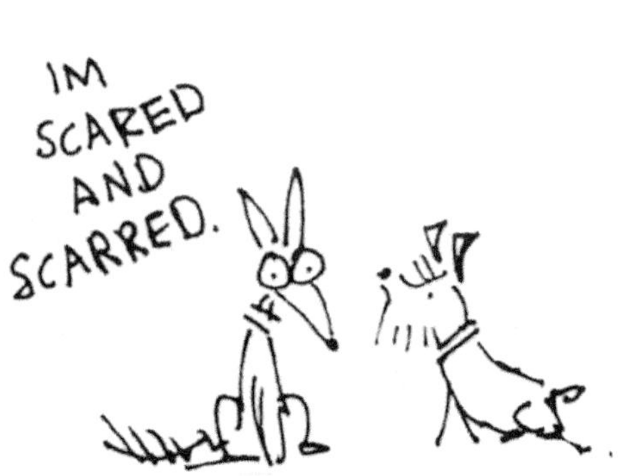
IM SCARED AND SCARRED.

ES

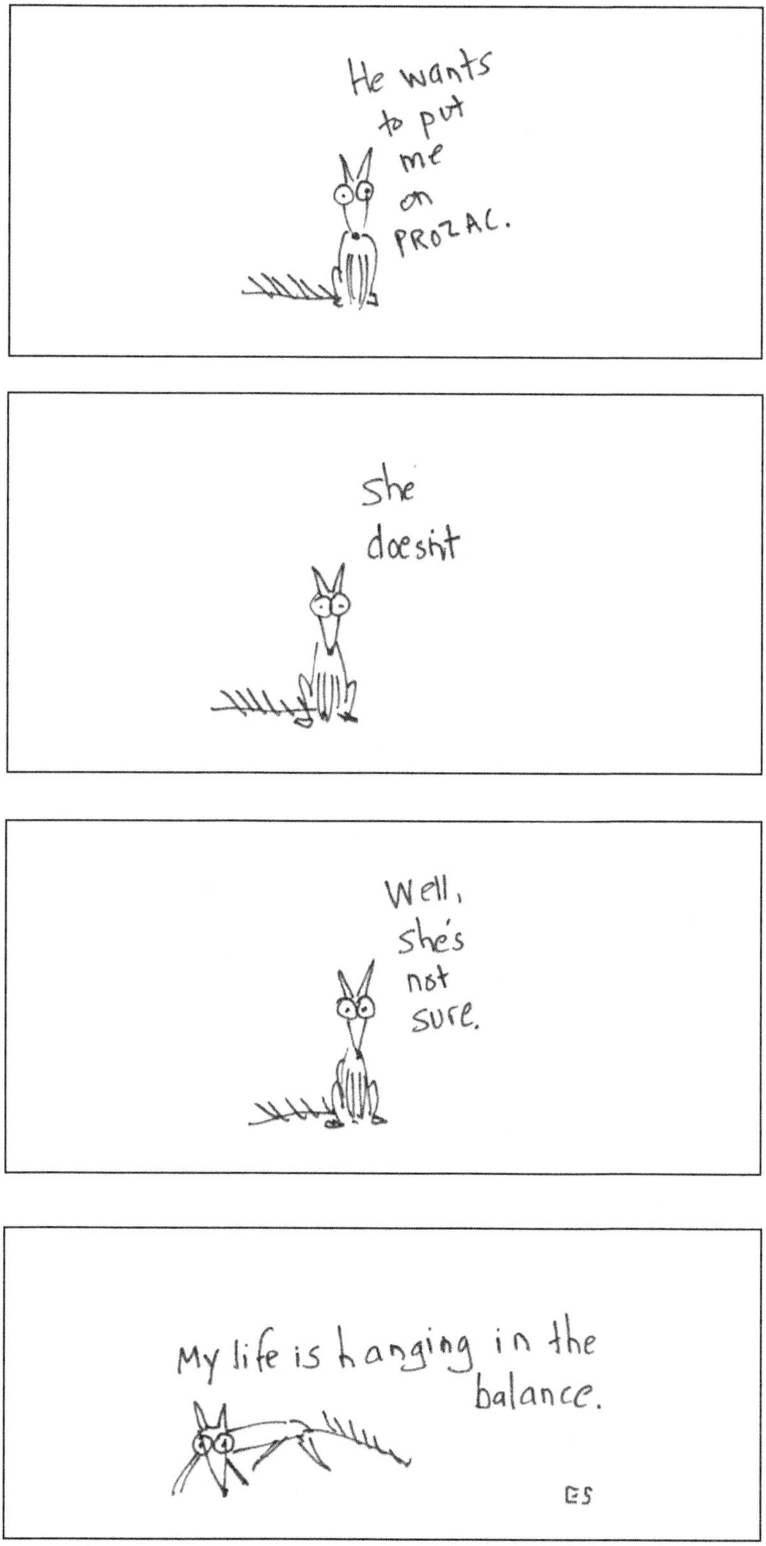
He wants to put me on PROZAC.
She doesn't
Well, she's not sure.
My life is hanging in the balance.
ES

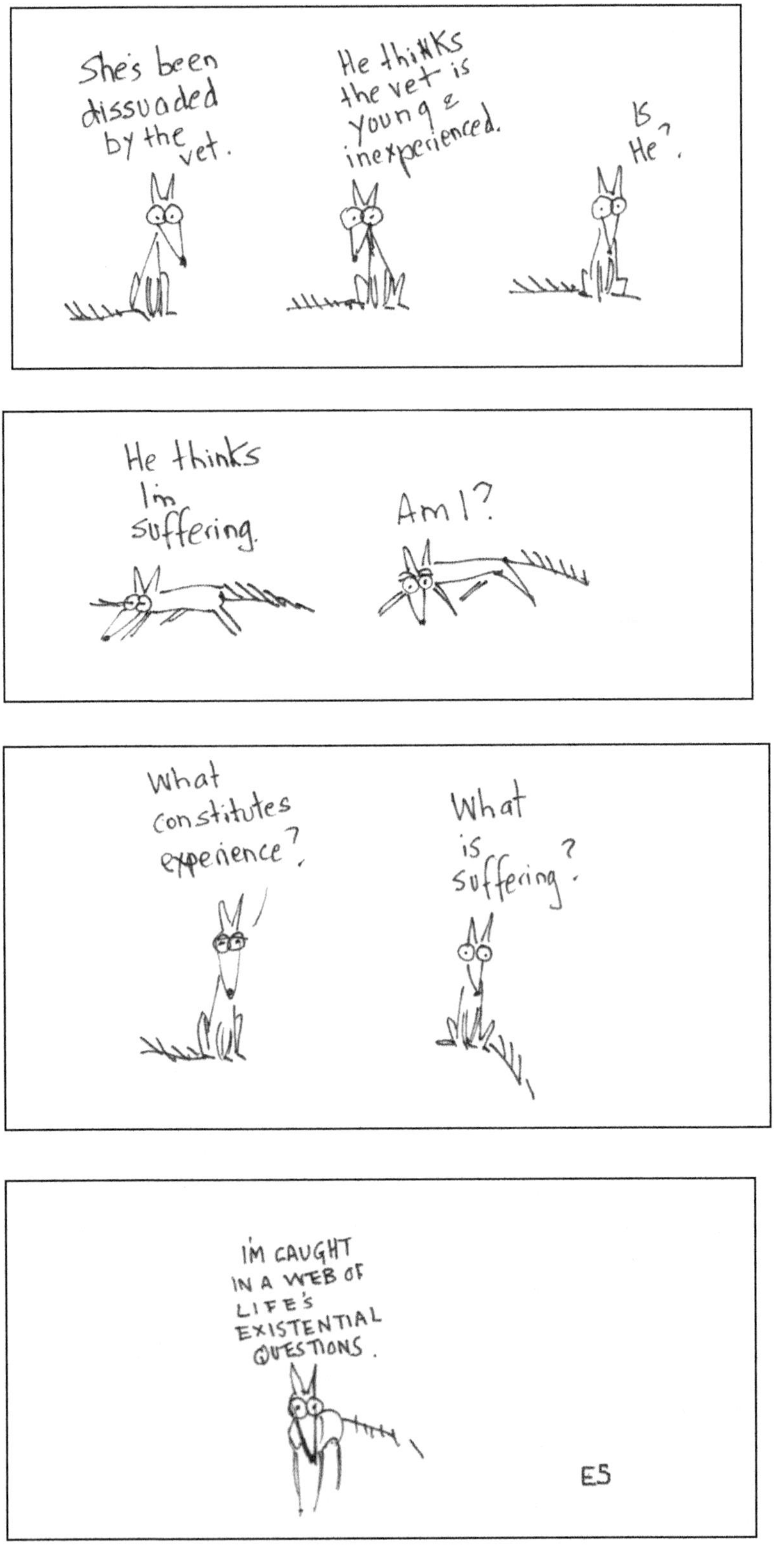
She's been dissuaded by the vet.
He thinks the vet is young & inexperienced.
Is He?
He thinks I'm suffering.
Am I?
What constitutes experience?
What is suffering?
I'M CAUGHT IN A WEB OF LIFE'S EXISTENTIAL QUESTIONS.
ES

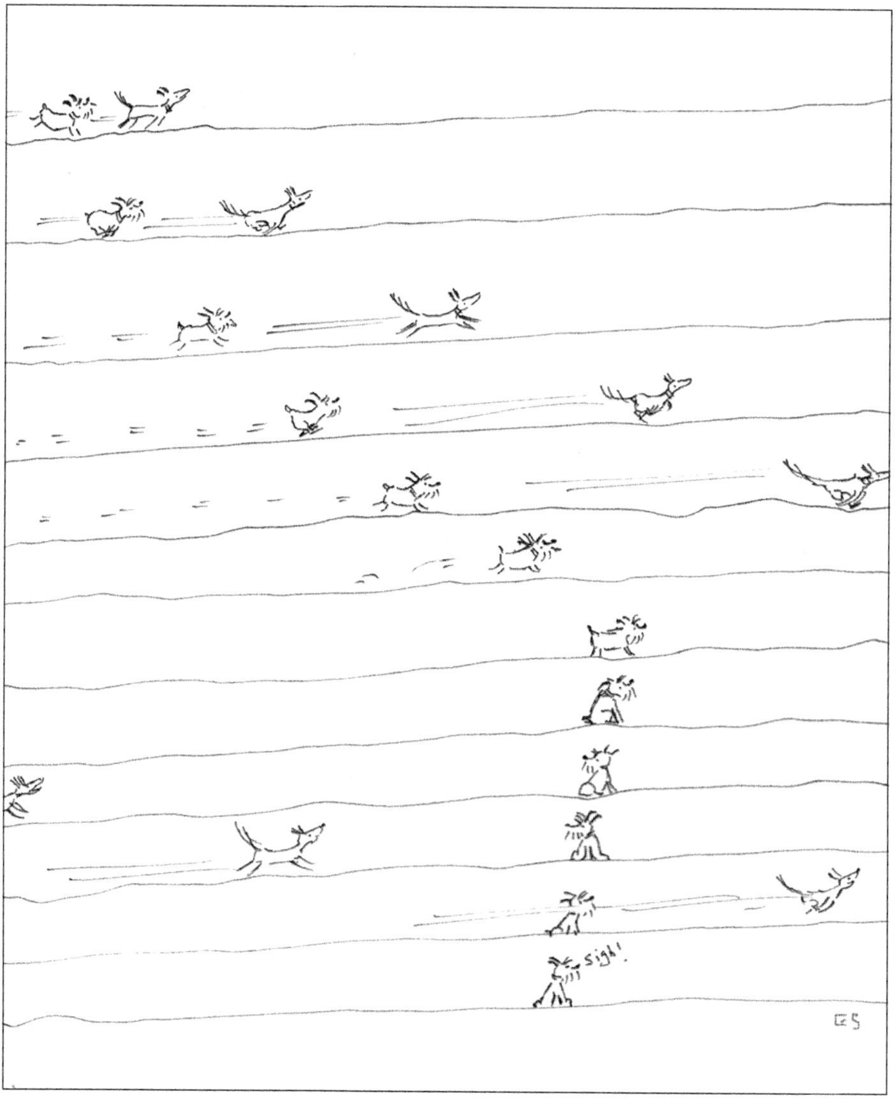
sigh!
GS

I'M FEELING
REALLY HAPPY!
THE PROZAC
IS WORKING!
YOU'RE NOT ON PROZAC
I'M NOT?
NOPE
YOU MUST BE FEELING HAPPY ALL BY YOURSELF!
ALL BY MYSELF?
I'M WEIGHTED DOWN BY THE ENORMOUS RESPONSIBILITY
ES

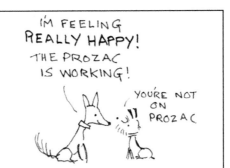

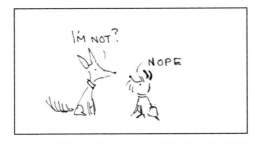

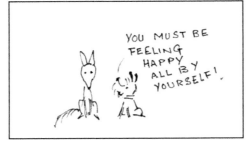

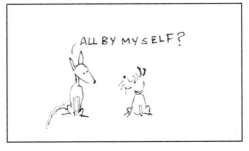

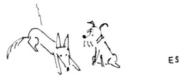

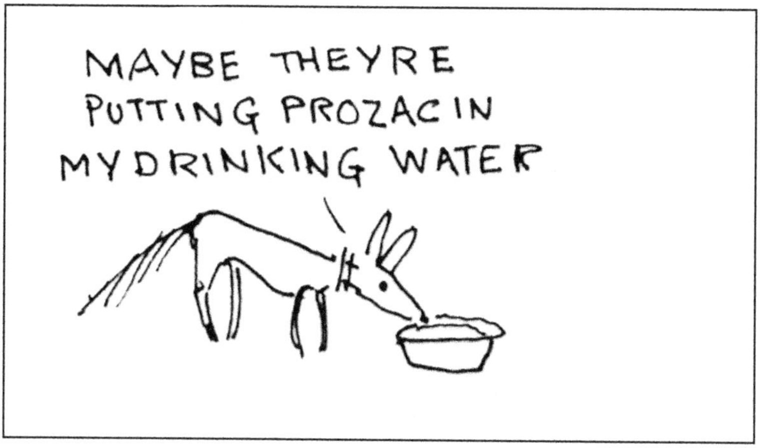
MAYBE THEYRE PUTTING PROZAC IN MY DRINKING WATER

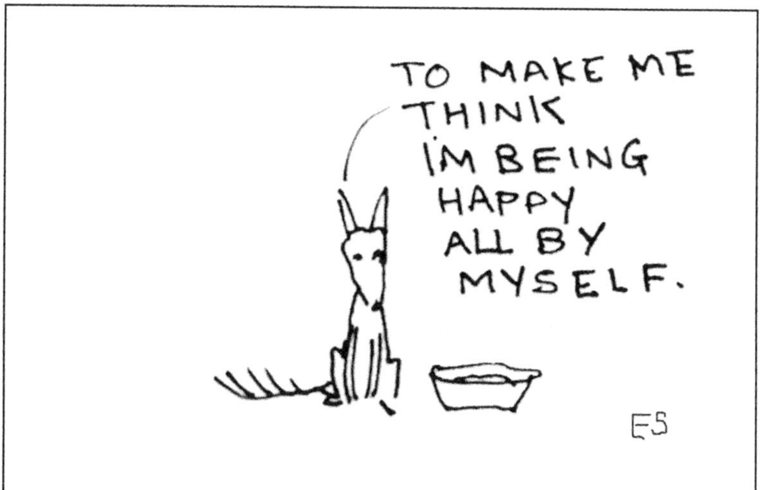
TO MAKE ME THINK I'M BEING HAPPY ALL BY MYSELF.
ES

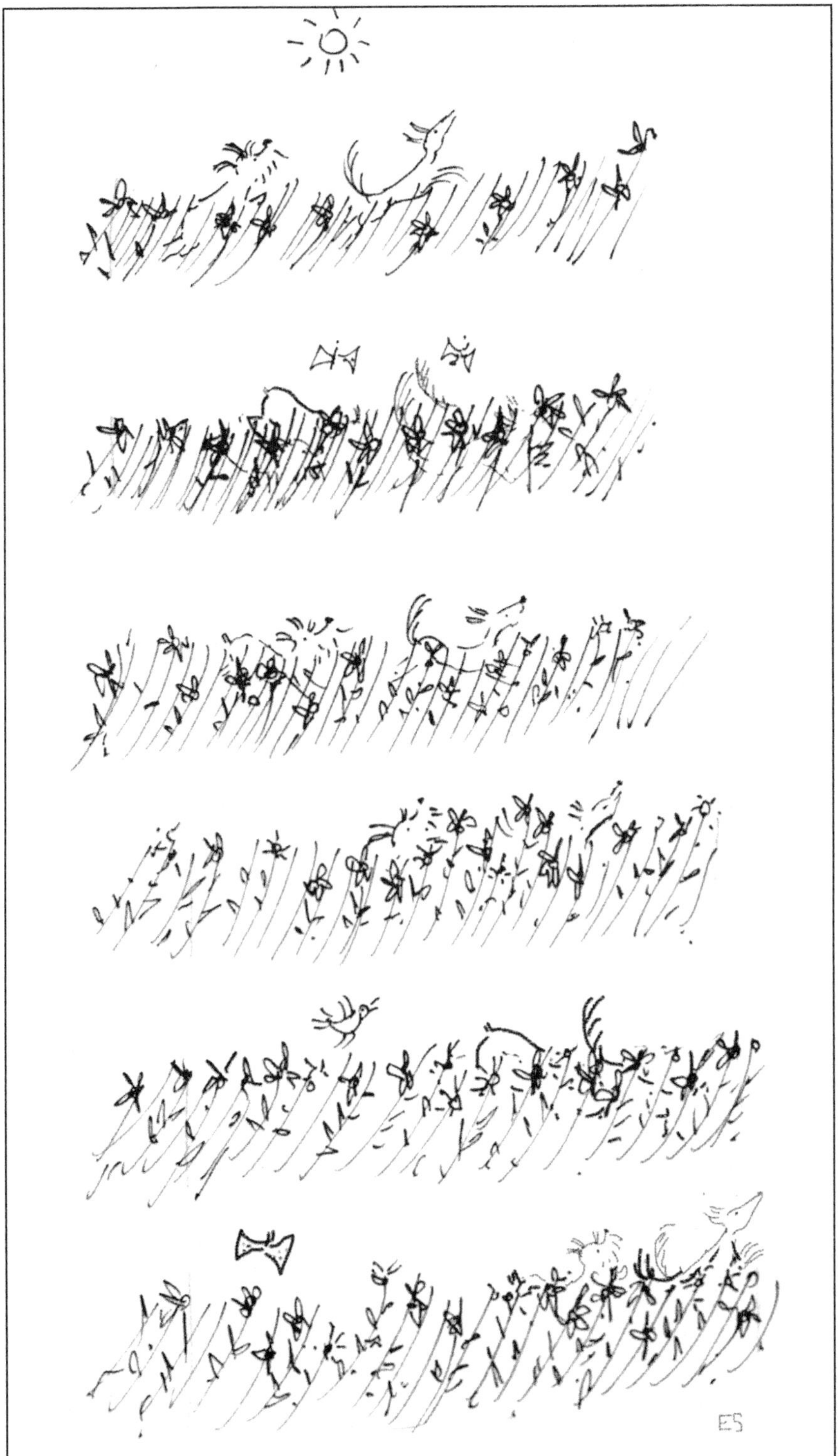
ES

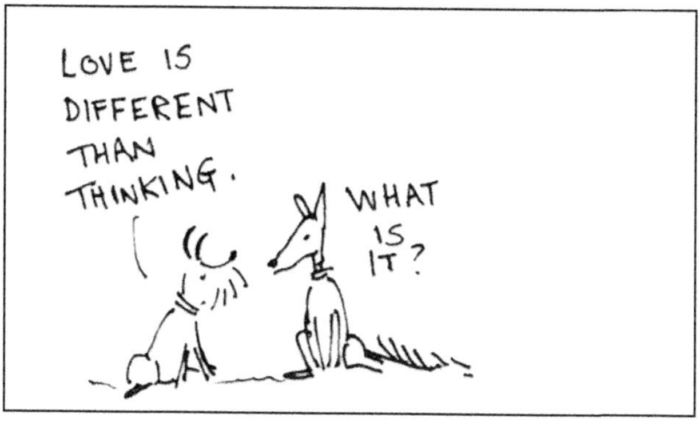
LOVE IS DIFFERENT THAN THINKING.
WHAT IS IT?

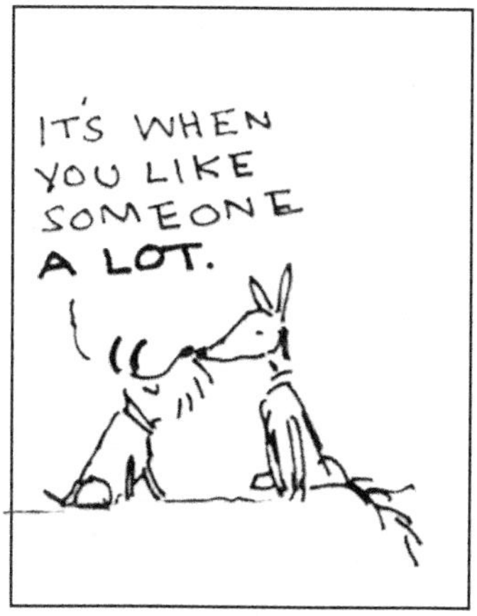
IT'S WHEN YOU LIKE SOMEONE **A LOT.**

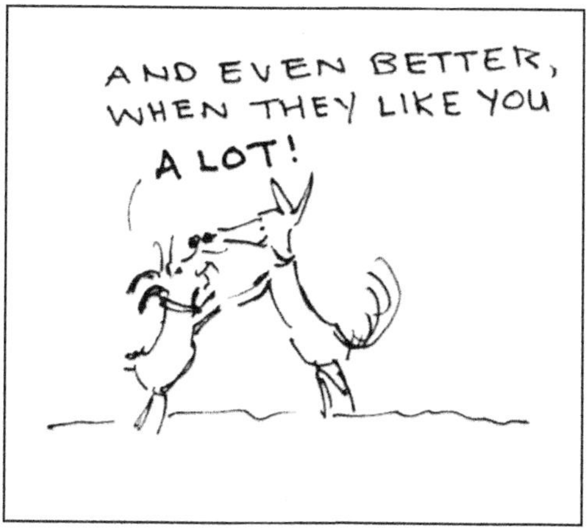
AND EVEN BETTER, WHEN THEY LIKE YOU **A LOT!**

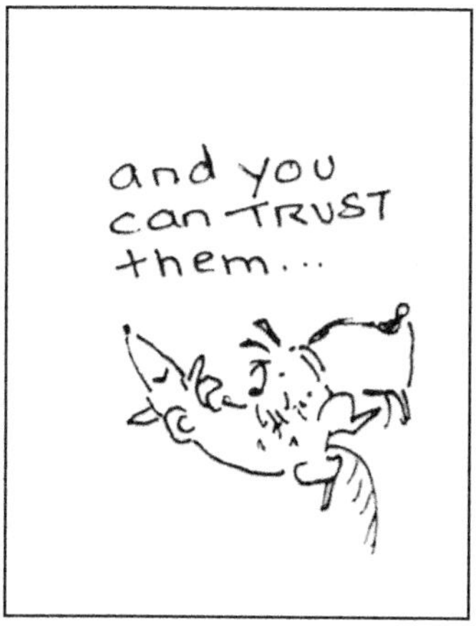
and you can TRUST them...

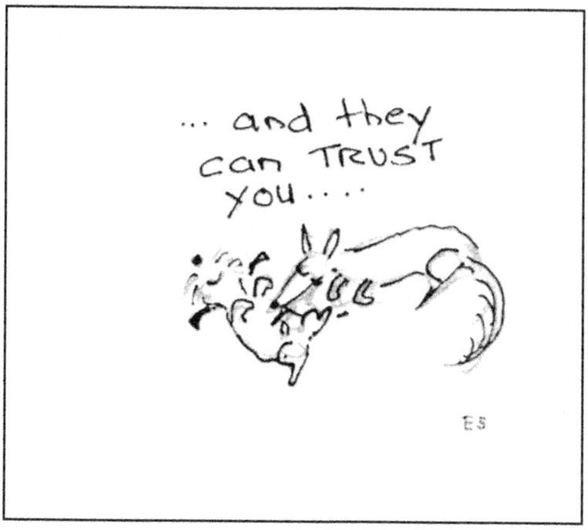
... and they can TRUST you....
ES

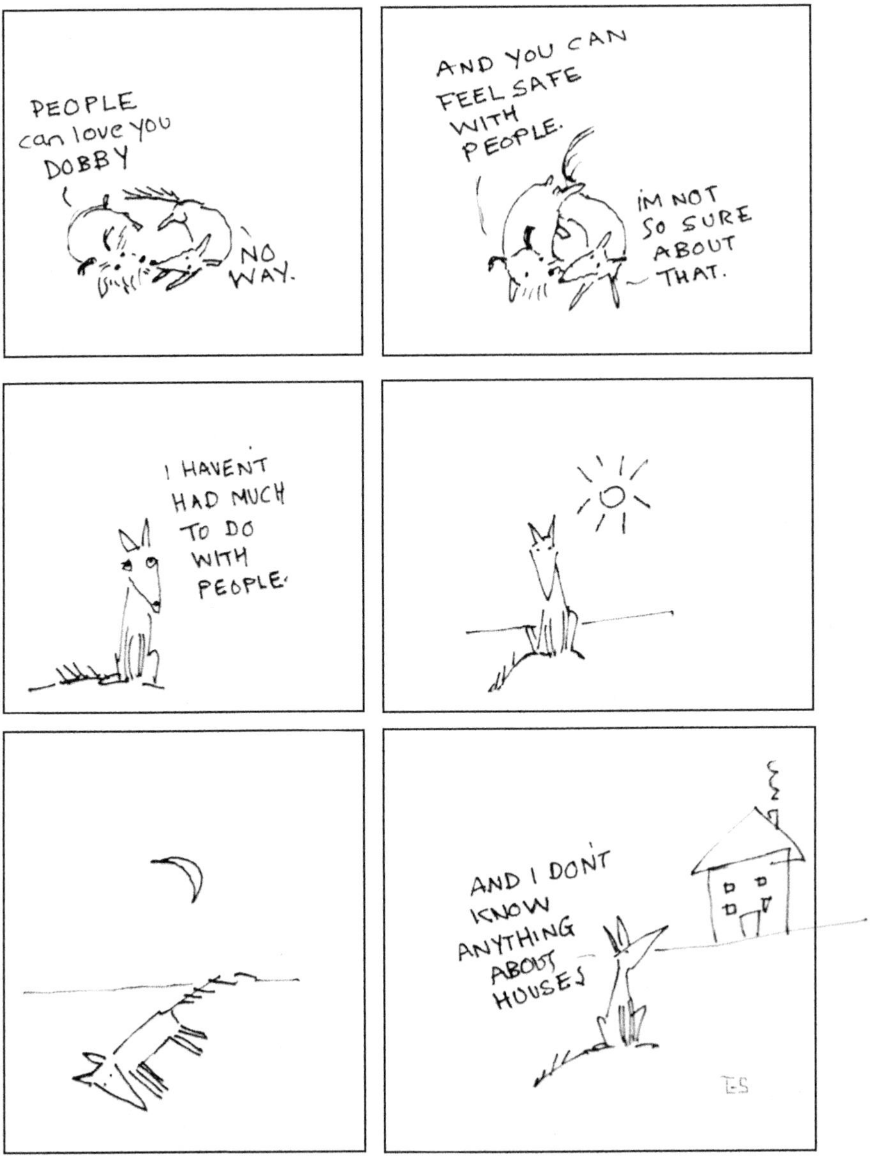
PEOPLE can love you DOBBY
NO WAY.
AND YOU CAN FEEL SAFE WITH PEOPLE.
IM NOT SO SURE ABOUT THAT.
I HAVENT HAD MUCH TO DO WITH PEOPLE.
AND I DONT KNOW ANYTHING ABOUT HOUSES
ES

WELL, NOW YOU ARE GOING TO LEARN ABOUT PEOPLE AND HOUSES.
I GUESS SO.
AND ABOUT LOVE
remember the most important bit Dobby.
WHAT?
LOVE IS DIFFERENT TO THINKING.

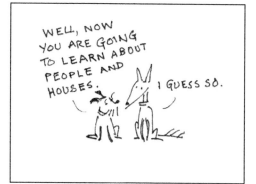

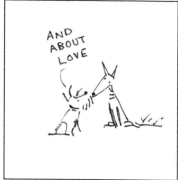

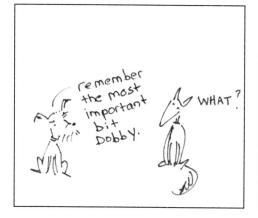

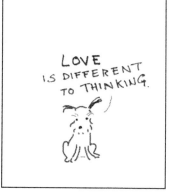

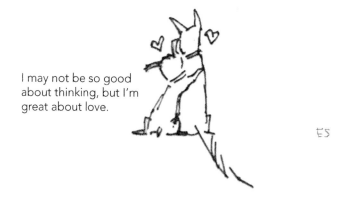

I may not be so good about thinking, but I'm great about love.

ES

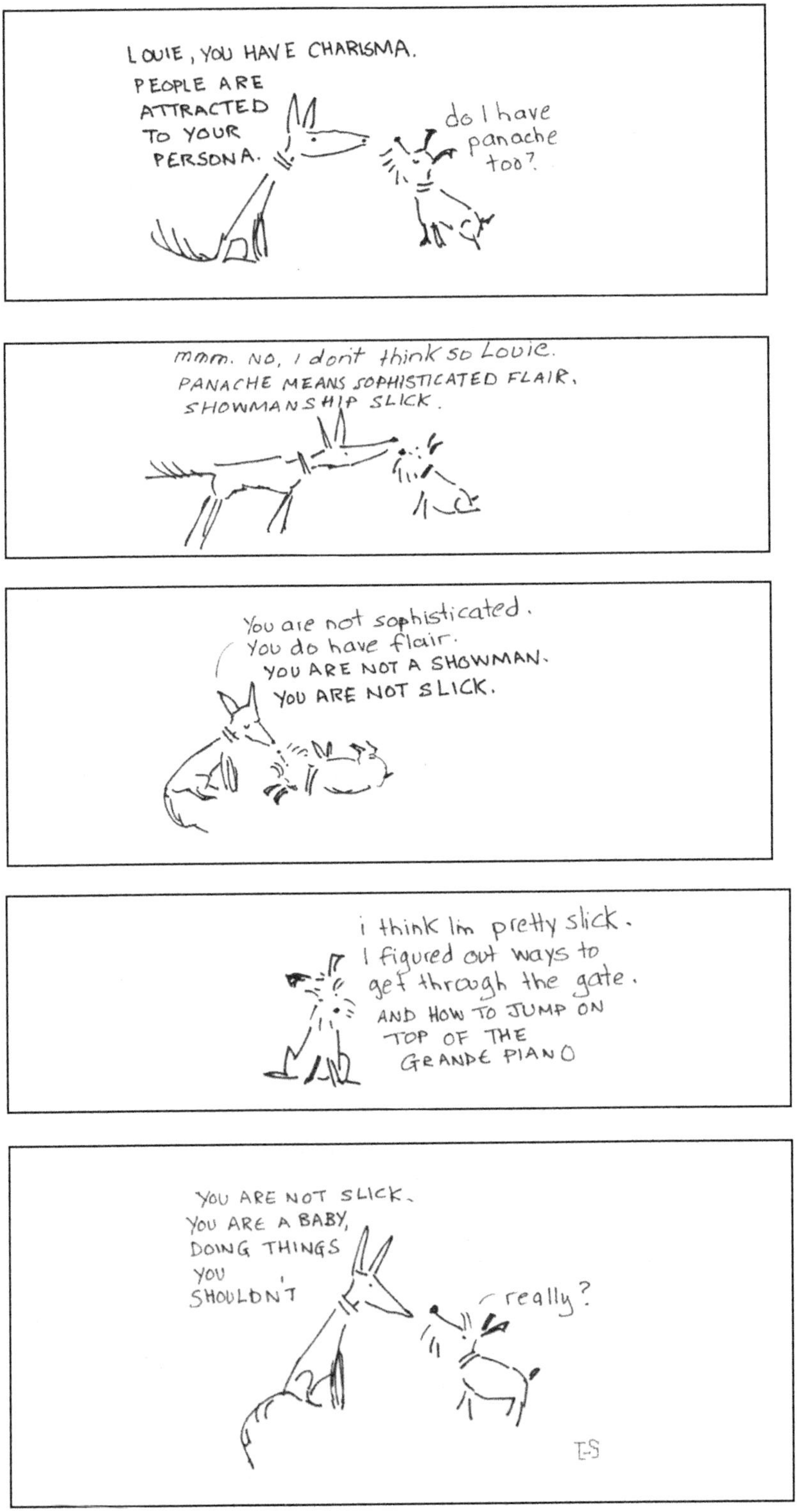
LOUIE, YOU HAVE CHARISMA.
PEOPLE ARE ATTRACTED TO YOUR PERSONA.
do I have panache too?
mmm. NO, I don't think so Louie.
PANACHE MEANS SOPHISTICATED FLAIR, SHOWMANSHIP SLICK.
You are not sophisticated.
You do have flair.
YOU ARE NOT A SHOWMAN.
YOU ARE NOT SLICK.
i think Im pretty slick.
I figured out ways to get through the gate.
AND HOW TO JUMP ON TOP OF THE GRANDE PIANO
YOU ARE NOT SLICK.
YOU ARE A BABY, DOING THINGS YOU SHOULDN'T
really?
E-S

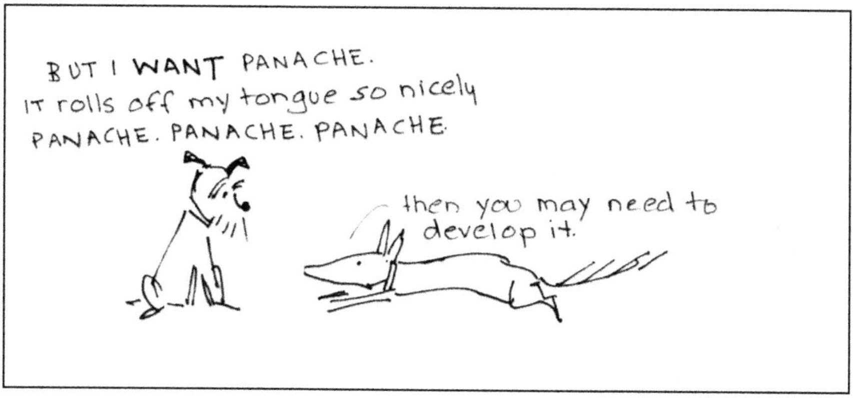
BUT I WANT PANACHE.
IT rolls off my tongue so nicely
PANACHE. PANACHE. PANACHE.
then you may need to develop it.

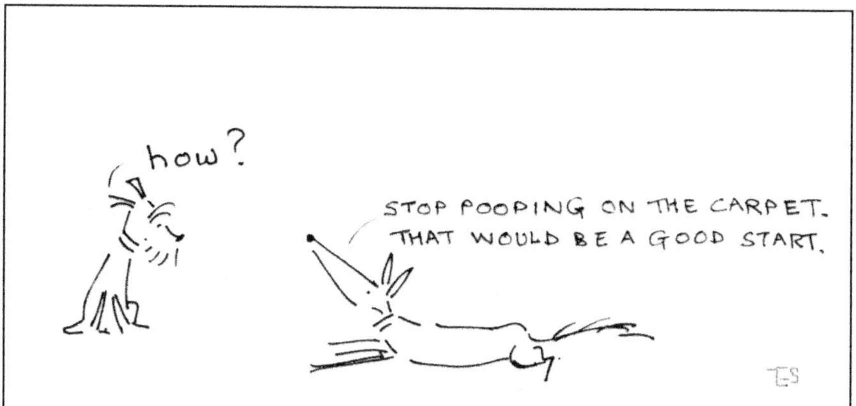
how?
STOP POOPING ON THE CARPET.
THAT WOULD BE A GOOD START.
TES

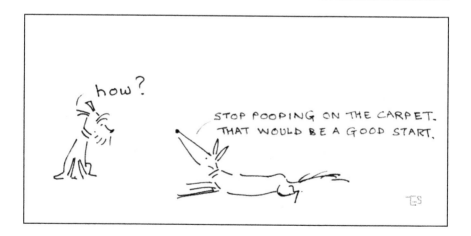

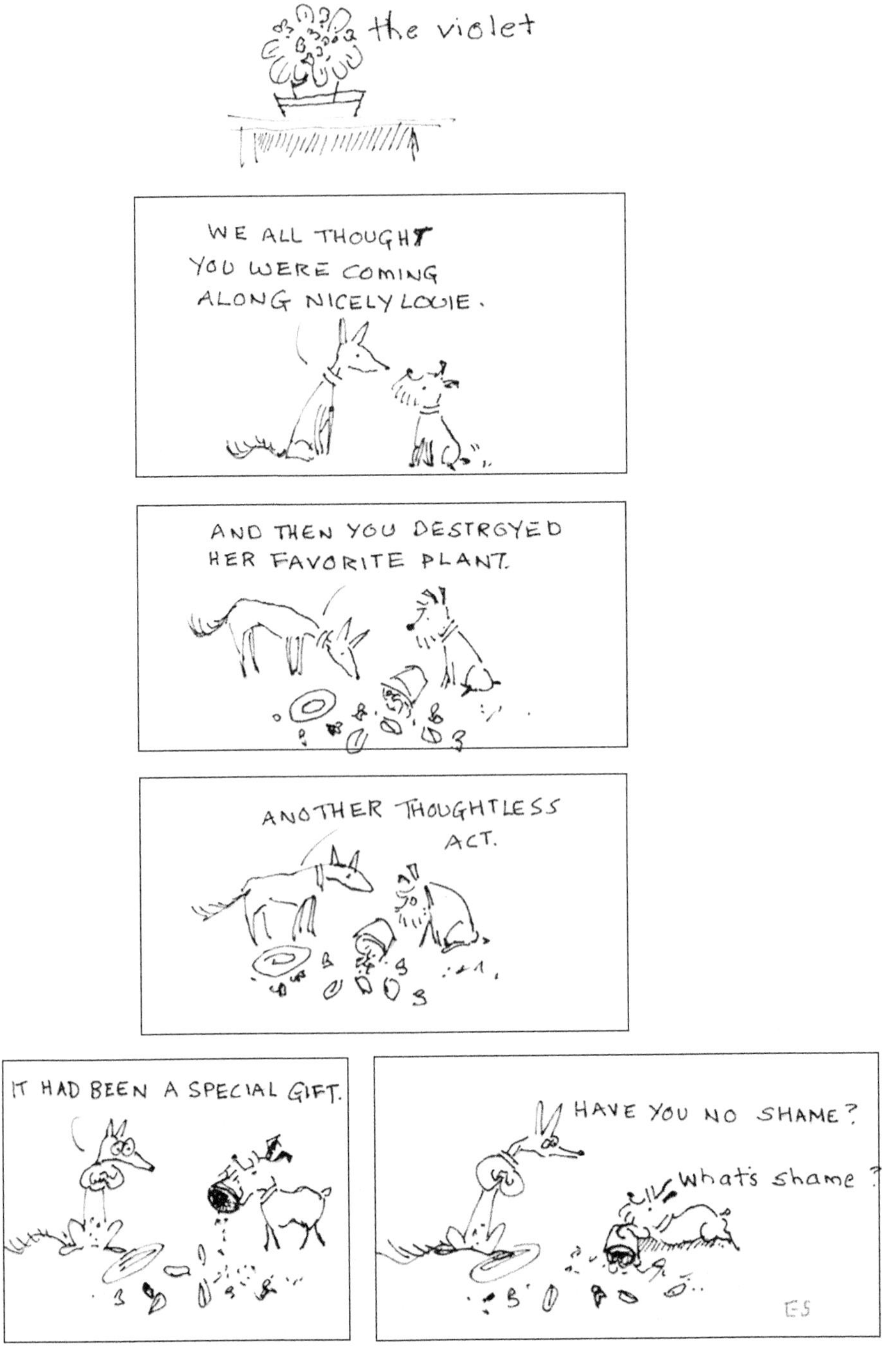
the violet
WE ALL THOUGHT YOU WERE COMING ALONG NICELY LOUIE.
AND THEN YOU DESTROYED HER FAVORITE PLANT.
ANOTHER THOUGHTLESS ACT.
IT HAD BEEN A SPECIAL GIFT.
HAVE YOU NO SHAME?
What's shame?
ES

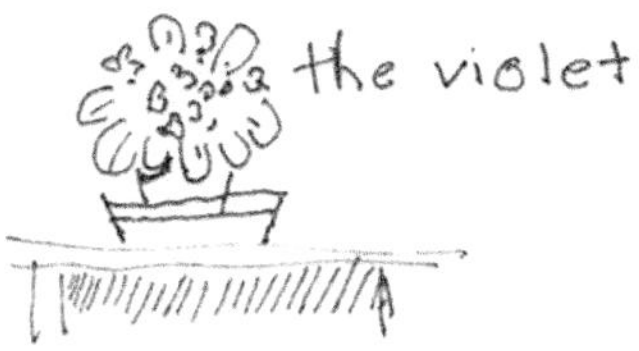
the violet

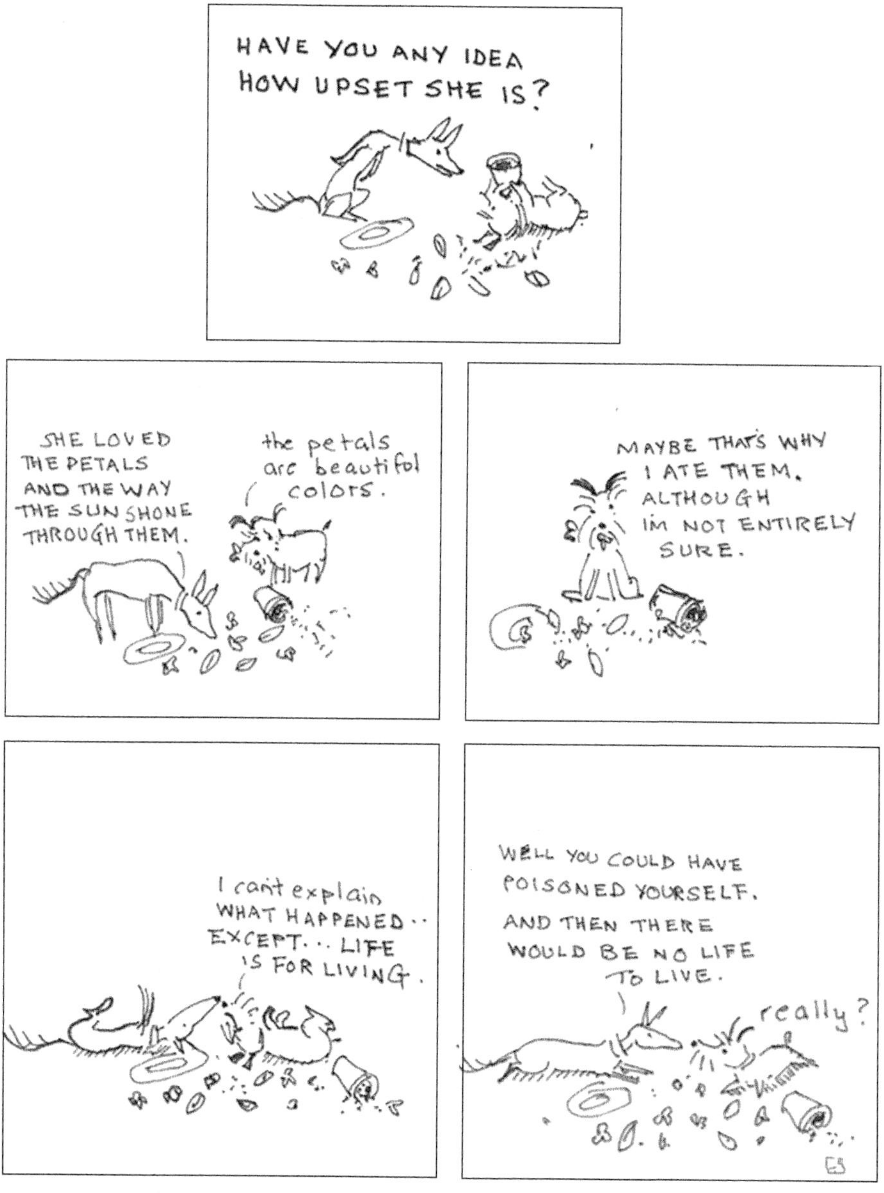
HAVE YOU ANY IDEA
HOW UPSET SHE IS?
SHE LOVED THE PETALS AND THE WAY THE SUN SHONE THROUGH THEM.
the petals are beautiful colors.
MAYBE THAT'S WHY I ATE THEM. ALTHOUGH I'M NOT ENTIRELY SURE.
I can't explain WHAT HAPPENED.. EXCEPT.. LIFE IS FOR LIVING.
WELL YOU COULD HAVE POISONED YOURSELF.
AND THEN THERE WOULD BE NO LIFE TO LIVE.
really?
ES

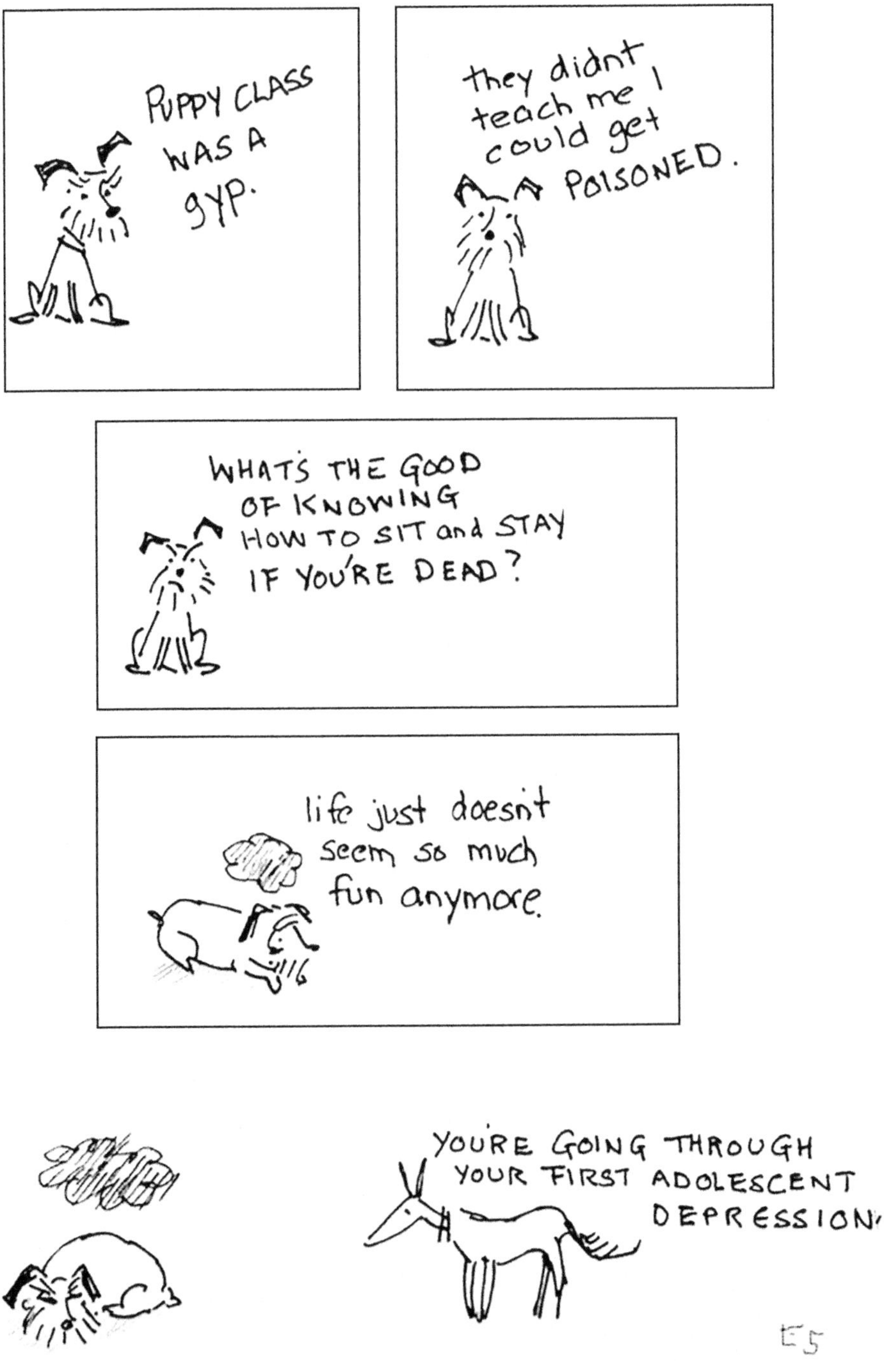
PUPPY CLASS WAS A GYP.
they didnt teach me I could get POISONED.
WHAT'S THE GOOD OF KNOWING HOW TO SIT and STAY IF YOU'RE DEAD?
life just doesn't seem so much fun anymore.
YOU'RE GOING THROUGH YOUR FIRST ADOLESCENT DEPRESSION.

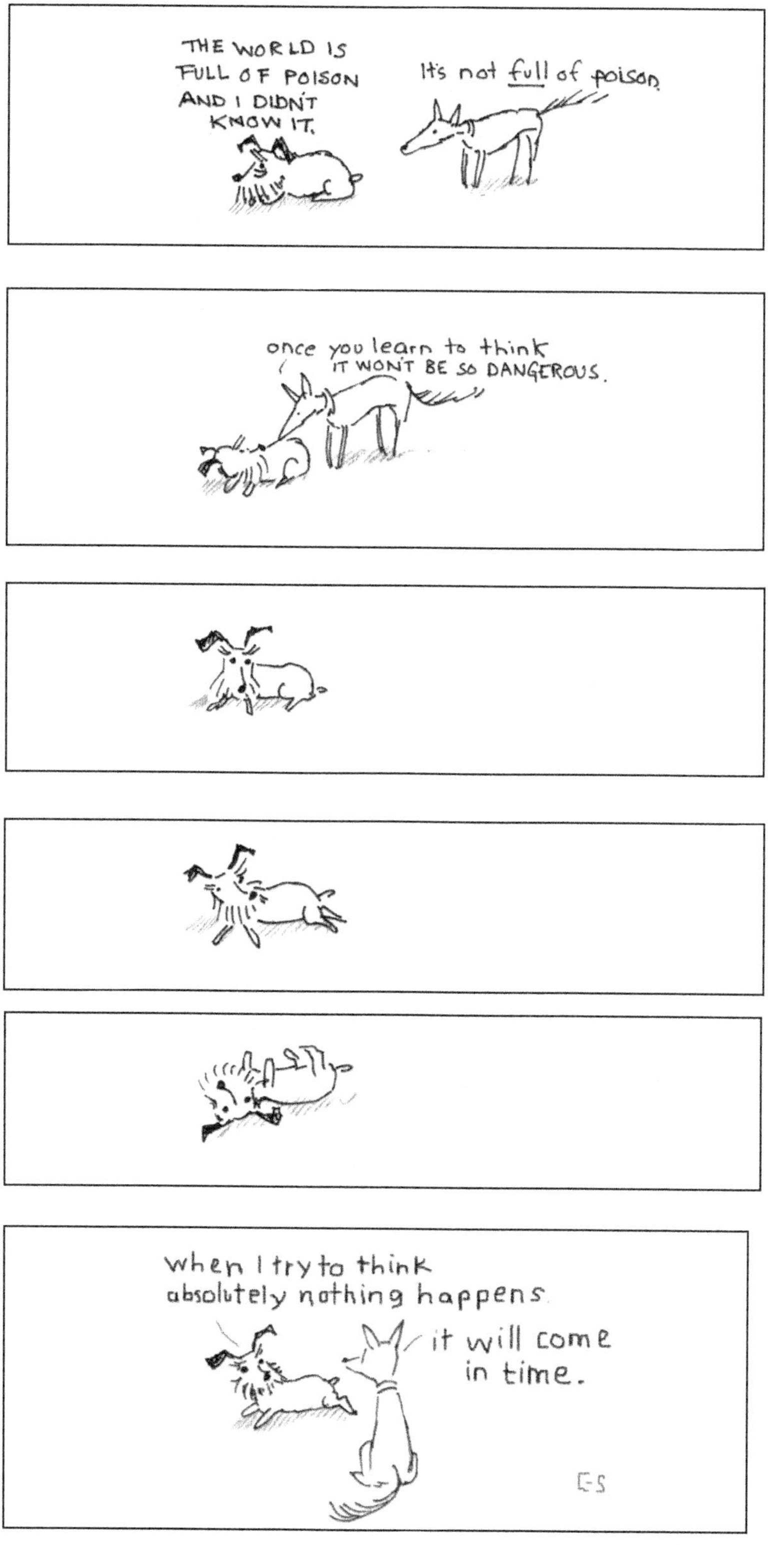
THE WORLD IS FULL OF POISON AND I DIDN'T KNOW IT.
It's not full of poison.
once you learn to think IT WON'T BE SO DANGEROUS.
when I try to think absolutely nothing happens
it will come in time.

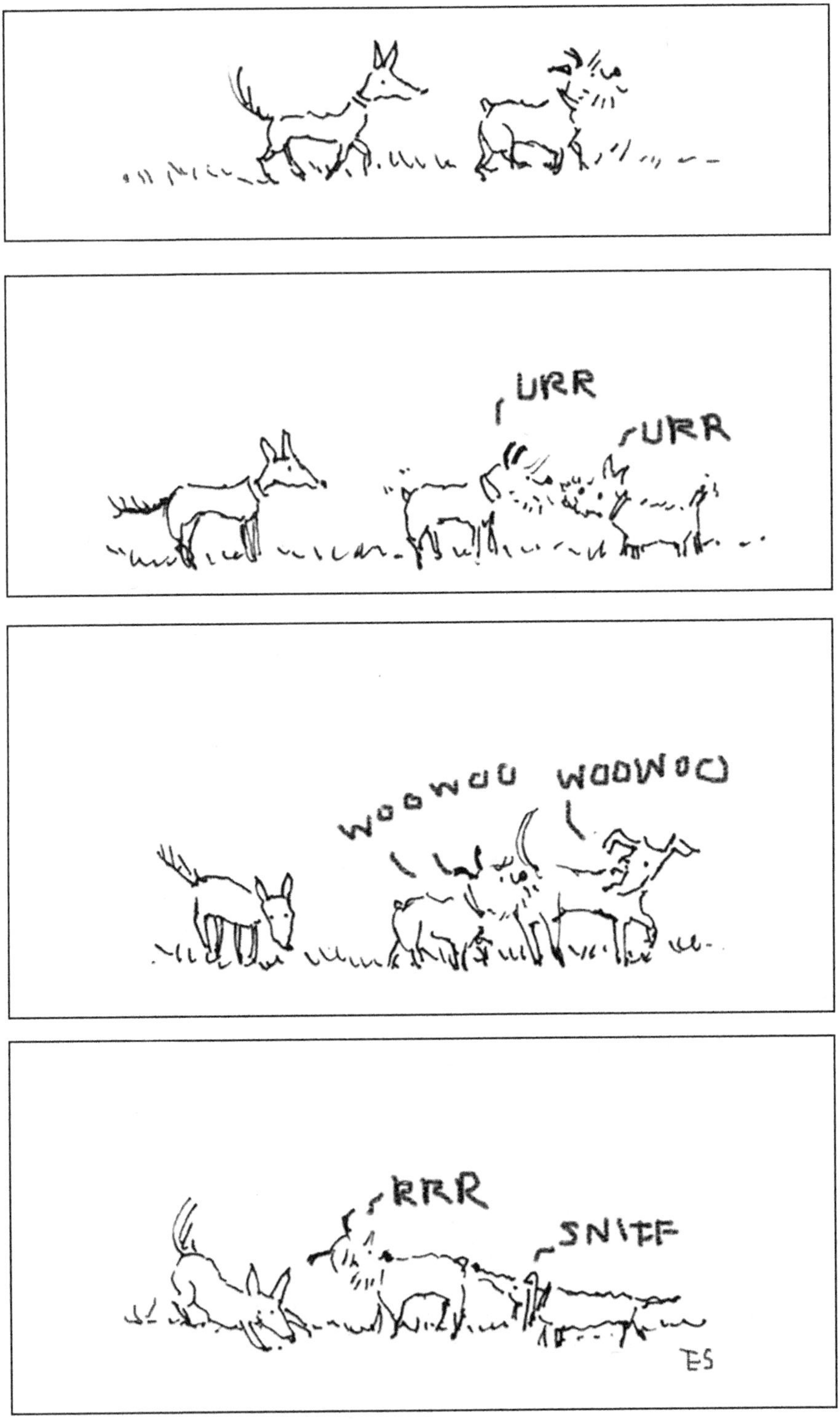
URR
URR
WOOWOO
WOOWOO
RRR
SNIFF
ES

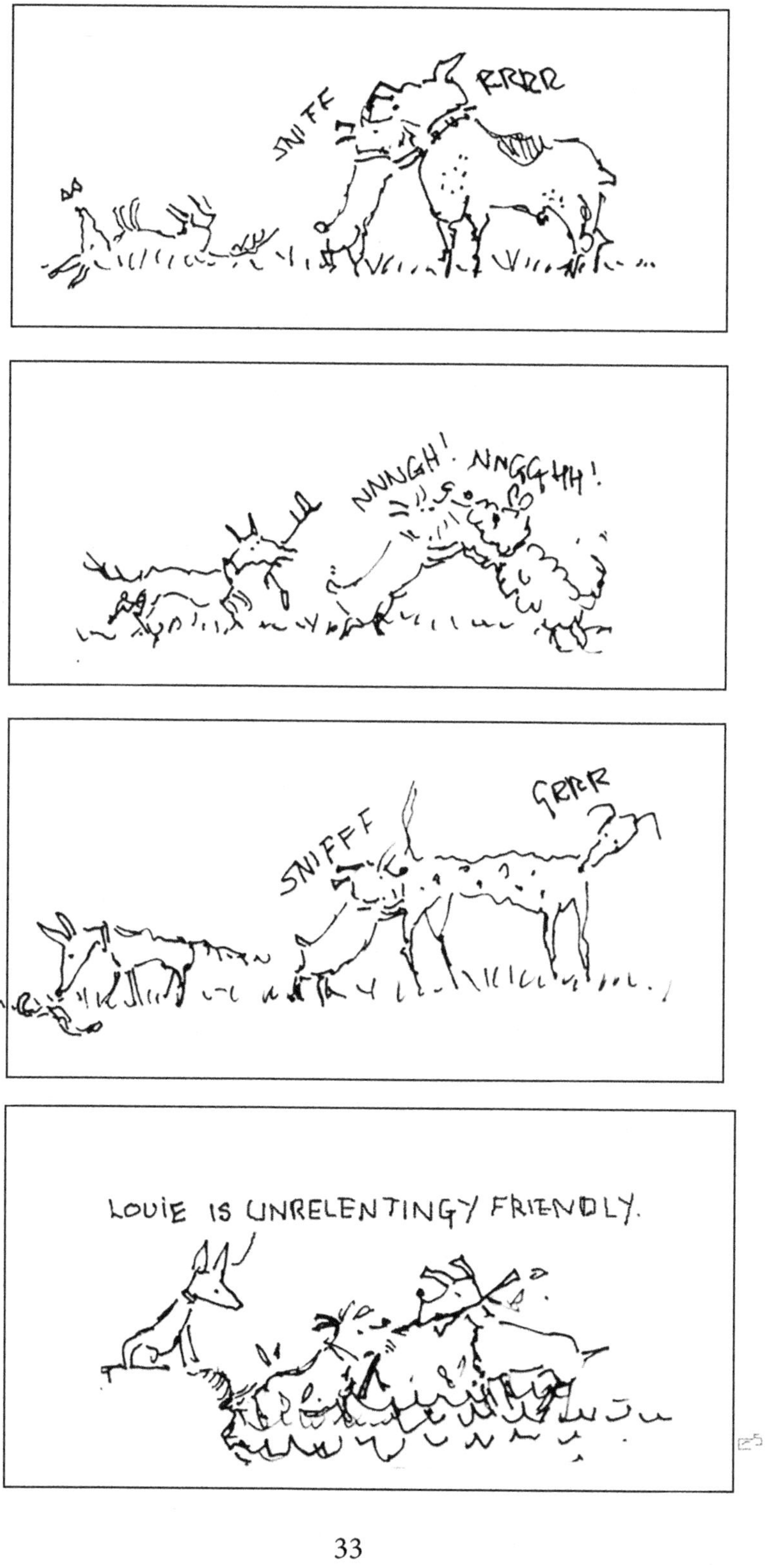
SNIFF
RRRR
NNNGH!
NNGGHH!
SNIFFF
GRRR
LOUIE IS UNRELENTINGY FRIENDLY.

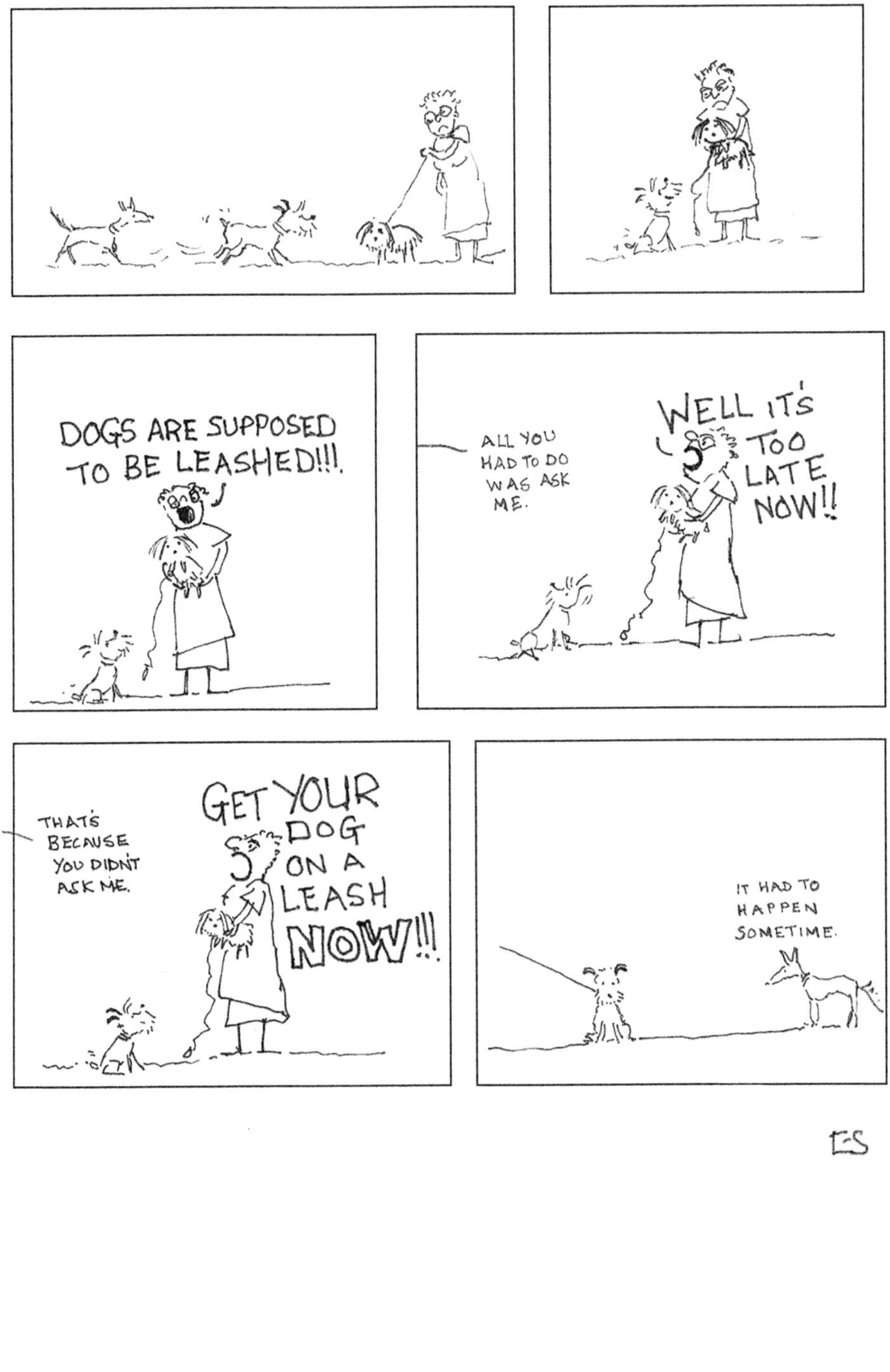
DOGS ARE SUPPOSED TO BE LEASHED!!!
ALL YOU HAD TO DO WAS ASK ME.
WELL IT'S TOO LATE NOW!!
THAT'S BECAUSE YOU DIDN'T ASK ME.
GET YOUR DOG ON A LEASH NOW!!!
IT HAD TO HAPPEN SOMETIME.
ES

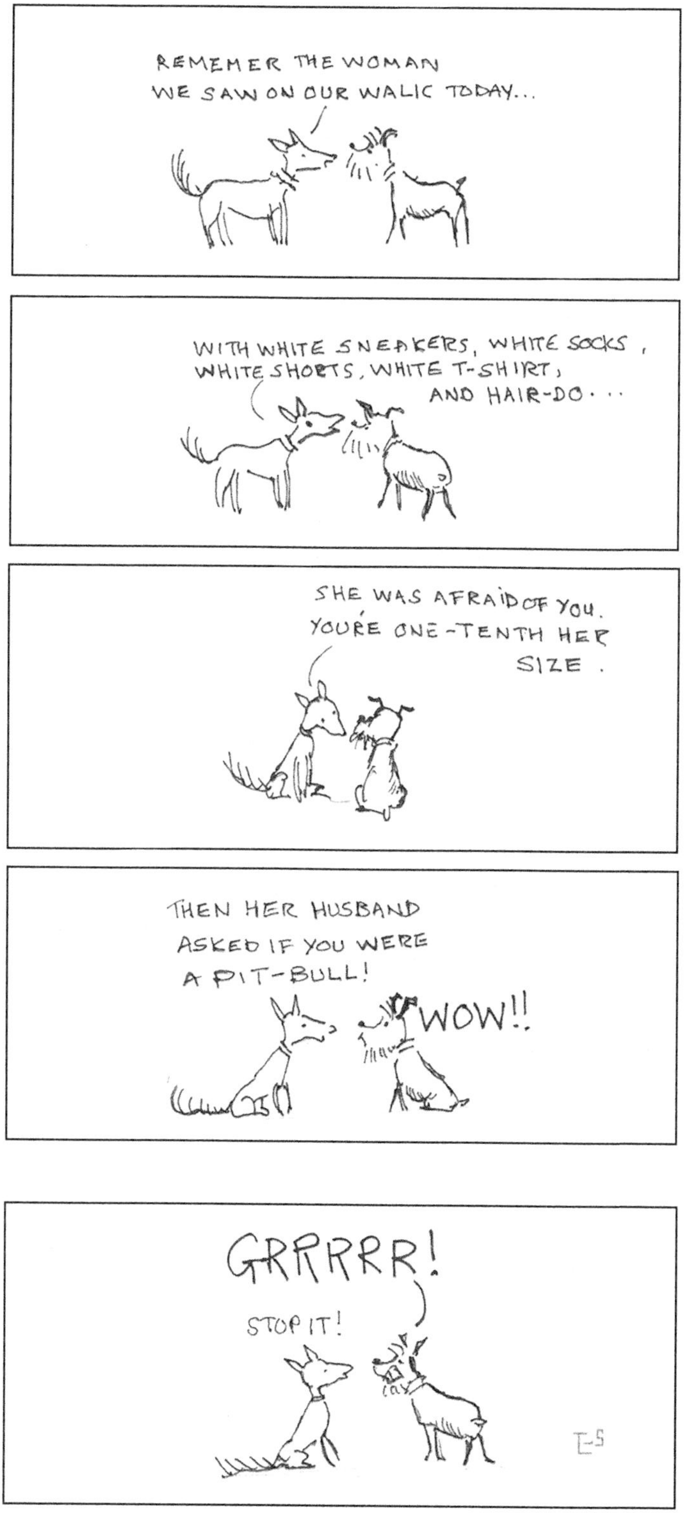
REMEMER THE WOMAN
WE SAW ON OUR WALK TODAY...
WITH WHITE SNEAKERS, WHITE SOCKS,
WHITE SHORTS, WHITE T-SHIRT,
AND HAIR-DO...
SHE WAS AFRAID OF YOU.
YOU'RE ONE-TENTH HER
SIZE.
THEN HER HUSBAND
ASKED IF YOU WERE
A PIT-BULL!
WOW!!
GRRRRR!
STOP IT!
E-S

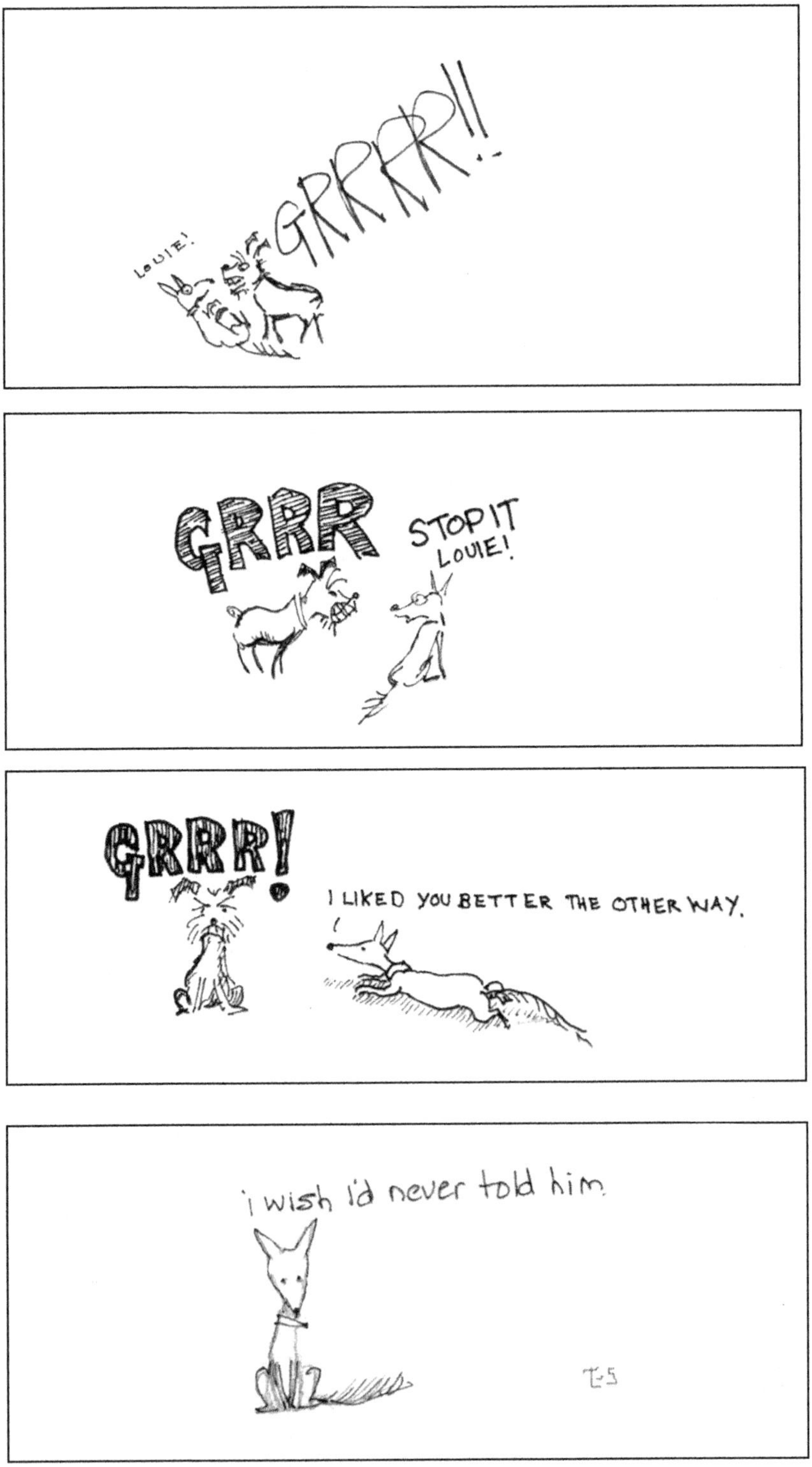
LOUIE!
GRRRR!!
GRRR
STOP IT LOUIE!
GRRR!
I LIKED YOU BETTER THE OTHER WAY.
i wish i'd never told him.
T-S

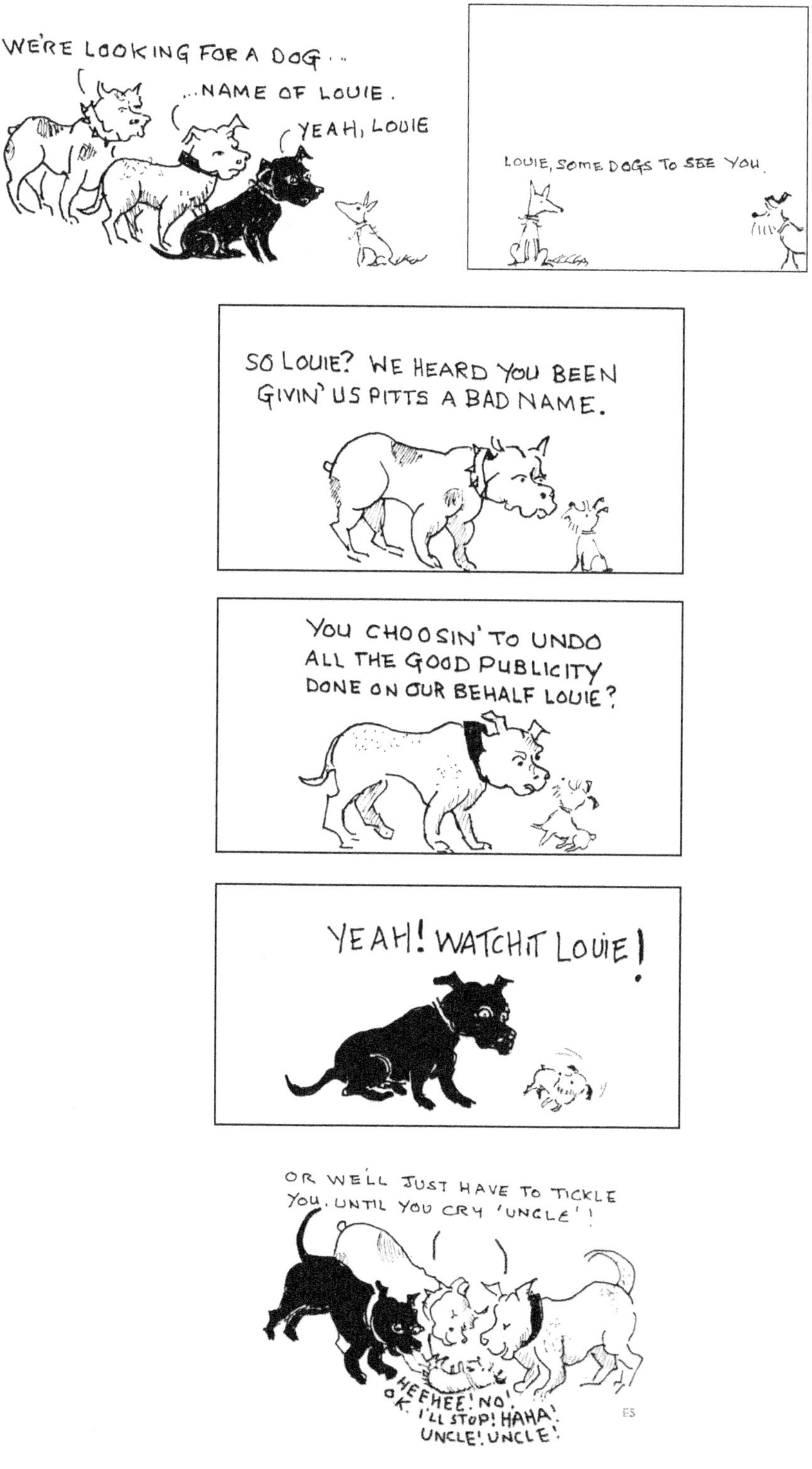
WE'RE LOOKING FOR A DOG...
...NAME OF LOUIE.
YEAH, LOUIE
LOUIE, SOME DOGS TO SEE YOU.
SO LOUIE? WE HEARD YOU BEEN GIVIN' US PITTS A BAD NAME.
YOU CHOOSIN' TO UNDO ALL THE GOOD PUBLICITY DONE ON OUR BEHALF LOUIE?
YEAH! WATCHIT LOUIE!
OR WE'LL JUST HAVE TO TICKLE YOU, UNTIL YOU CRY 'UNCLE'!
HEEHEE! NO!
O.K. I'LL STOP! HAHA!
UNCLE! UNCLE!
ES

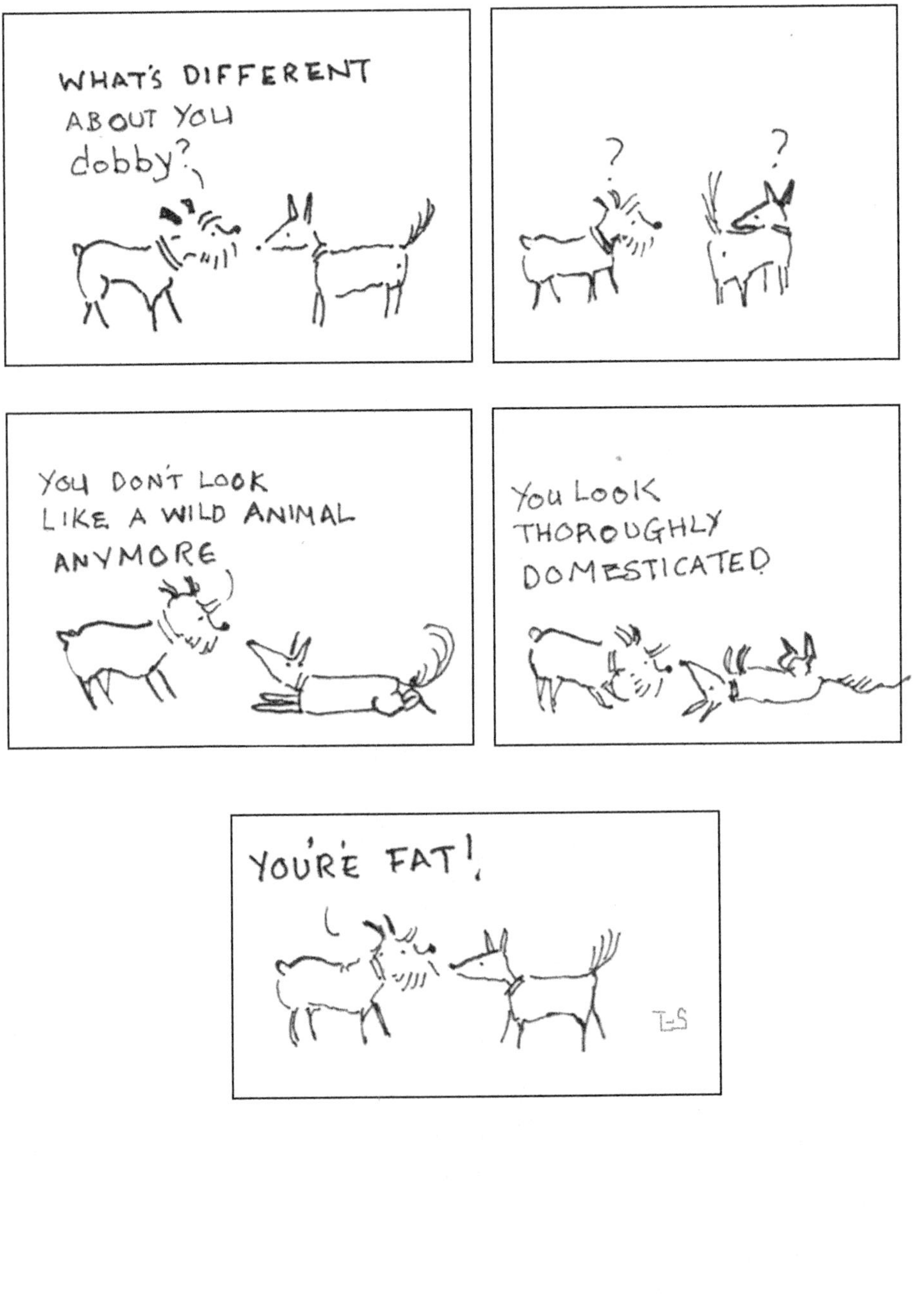
WHAT'S DIFFERENT ABOUT YOU dobby?
?
?
YOU DON'T LOOK LIKE A WILD ANIMAL ANYMORE
YOU LOOK THOROUGHLY DOMESTICATED
YOU'RE FAT!

THERE ARE ADVANTAGES TO LOUIE BEING AN EXTROVERT.

HE'S TOO EXCITED ABOUT EACH NEW DAY....

... TO REMEMBER TO EAT HIS FOOD ..

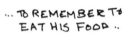

AND NOW THAT I AM NOT AFRAID OF FOOD BOWLS ANYMORE.

I GET DOUBLE HELPINGS.

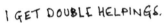

LOUIE, DOESN'T NOTICE....

BECAUSE HIS LIFE IS FULL OF WONDERFUL DISTRACTIONS.

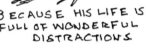

BURP! LIFE IS GOOD!

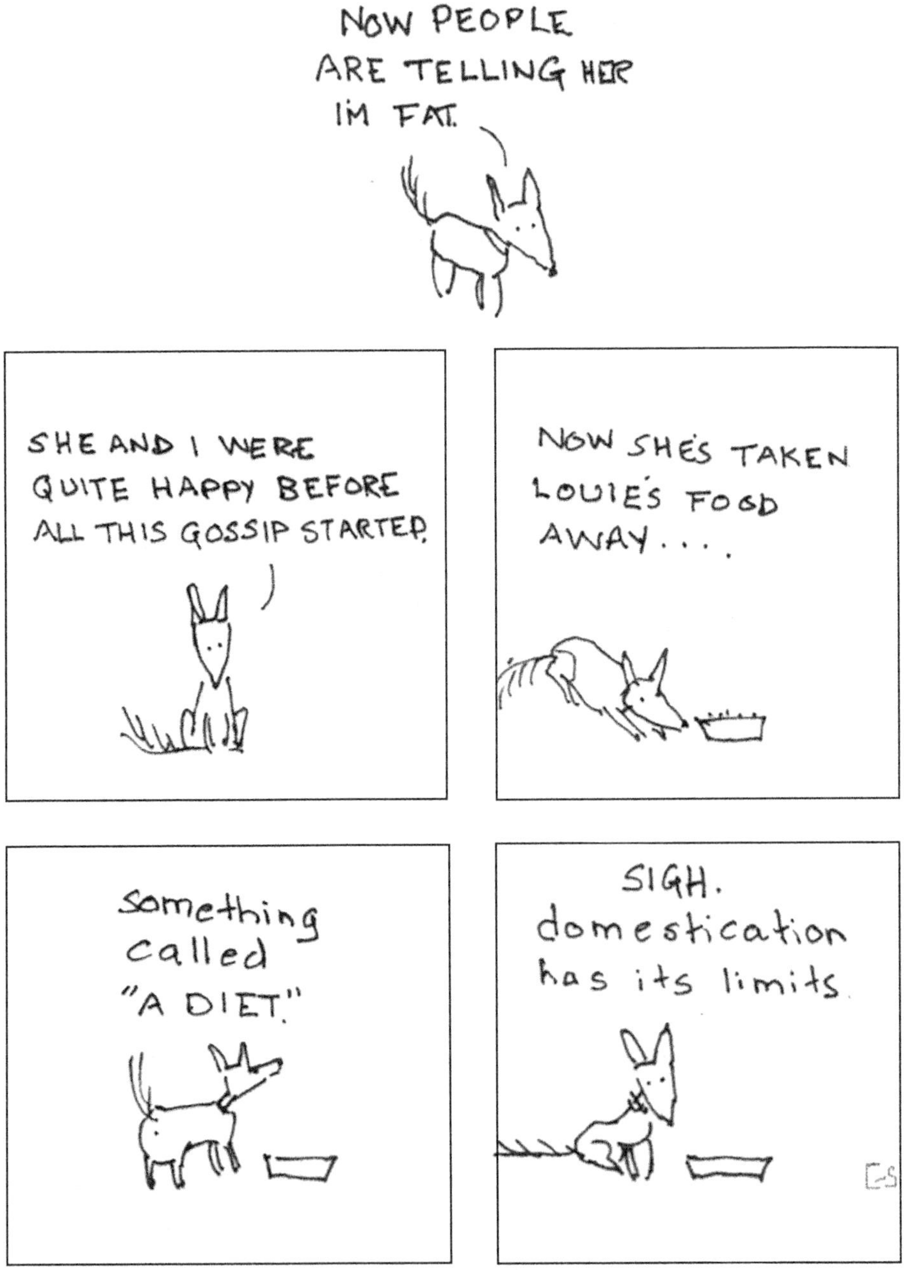

NOW PEOPLE ARE TELLING HER IM FAT.
SHE AND I WERE QUITE HAPPY BEFORE ALL THIS GOSSIP STARTED
NOW SHE'S TAKEN LOUIE'S FOOD AWAY....
something called "A DIET."
SIGH. domestication has its limits.

the door

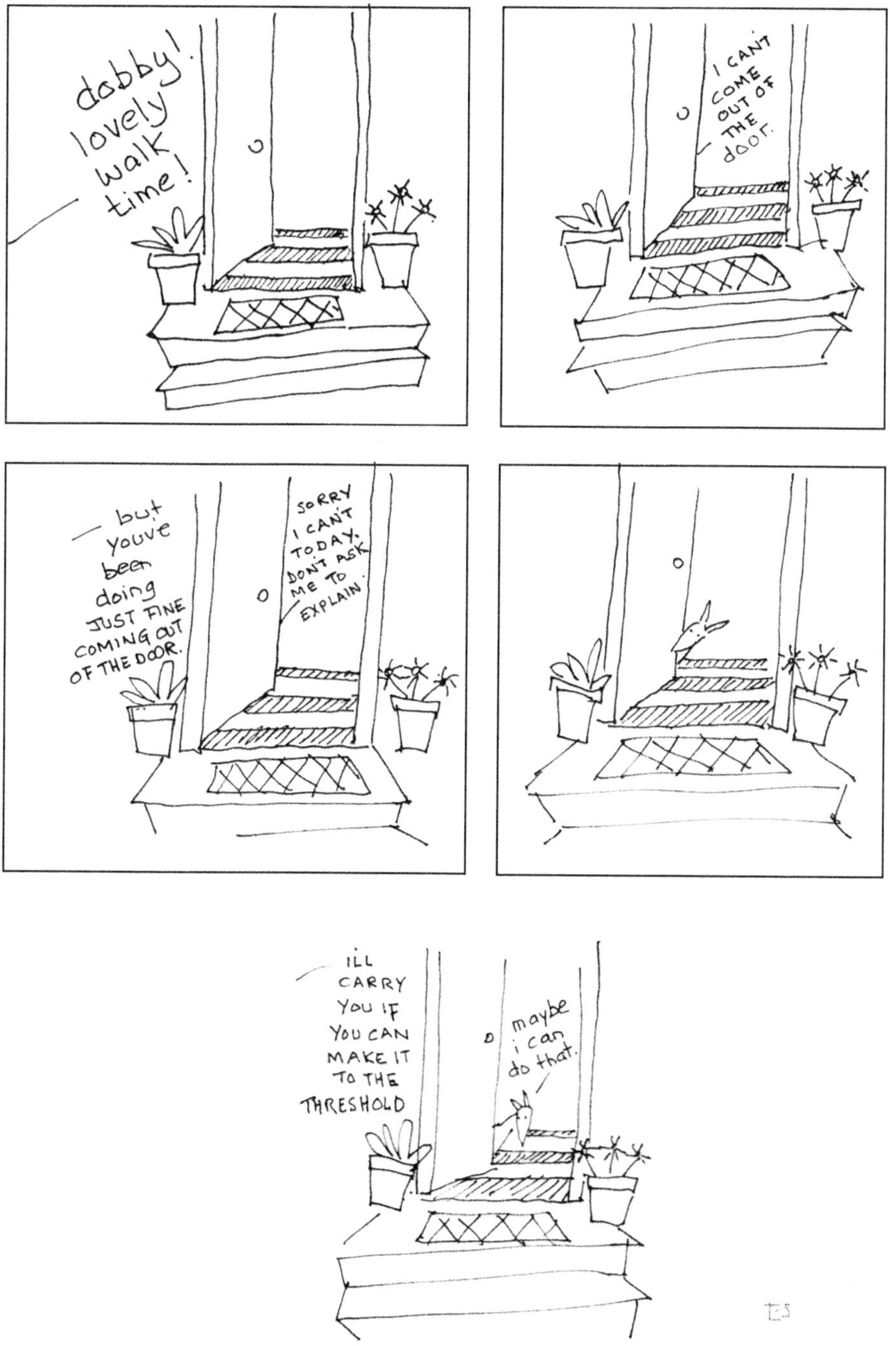
dobby! lovely walk time!
I CAN'T COME OUT OF THE door.
but youve been doing JUST FINE COMING OUT OF THE DOOR.
SORRY I CAN'T TODAY. DON'T ASK ME TO EXPLAIN.
ILL CARRY YOU IF YOU CAN MAKE IT TO THE THRESHOLD
maybe i can do that.

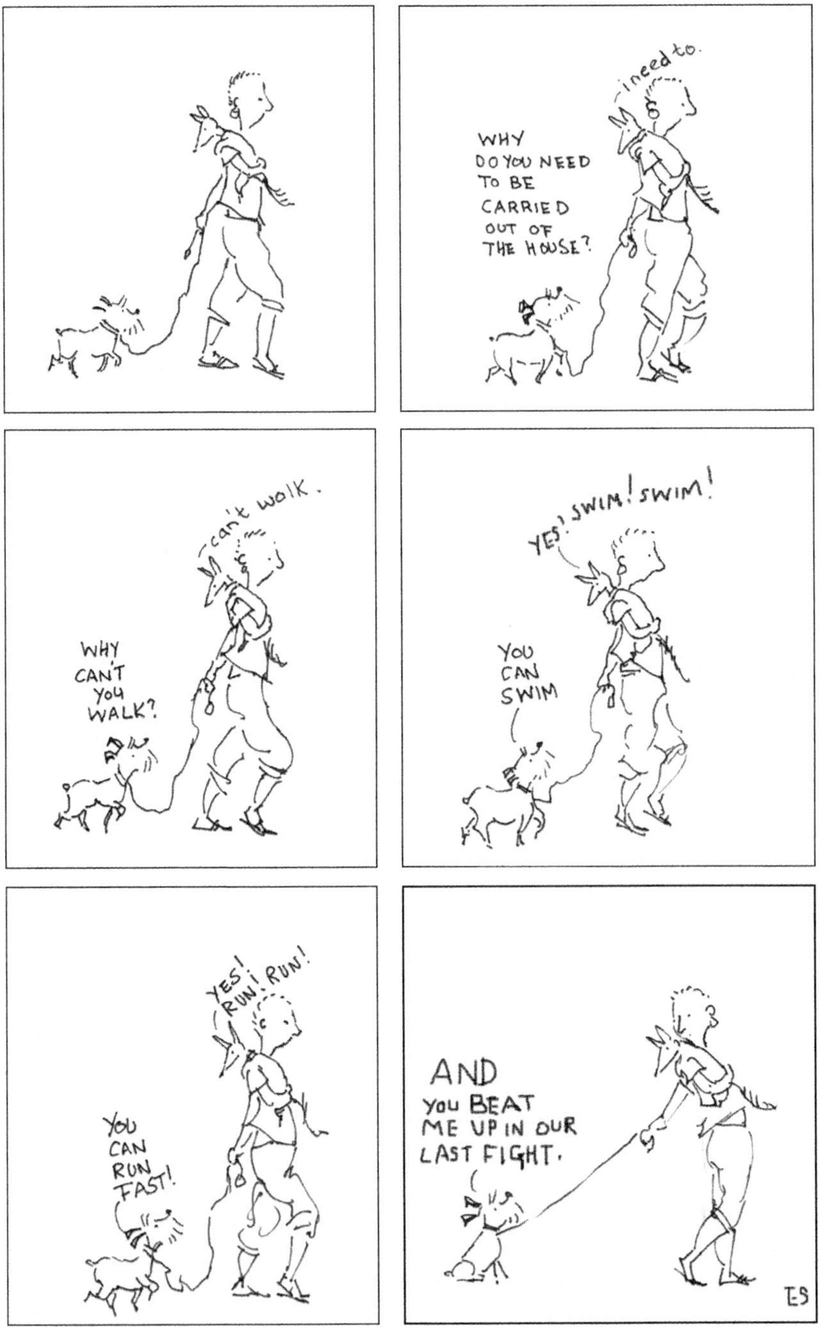
WHY DO YOU NEED TO BE CARRIED OUT OF THE HOUSE?
i need to.
WHY CAN'T YOU WALK?
can't walk.
YOU CAN SWIM
YES! SWIM! SWIM!
YOU CAN RUN FAST!
YES! RUN! RUN!
AND YOU BEAT ME UP IN OUR LAST FIGHT.
ES

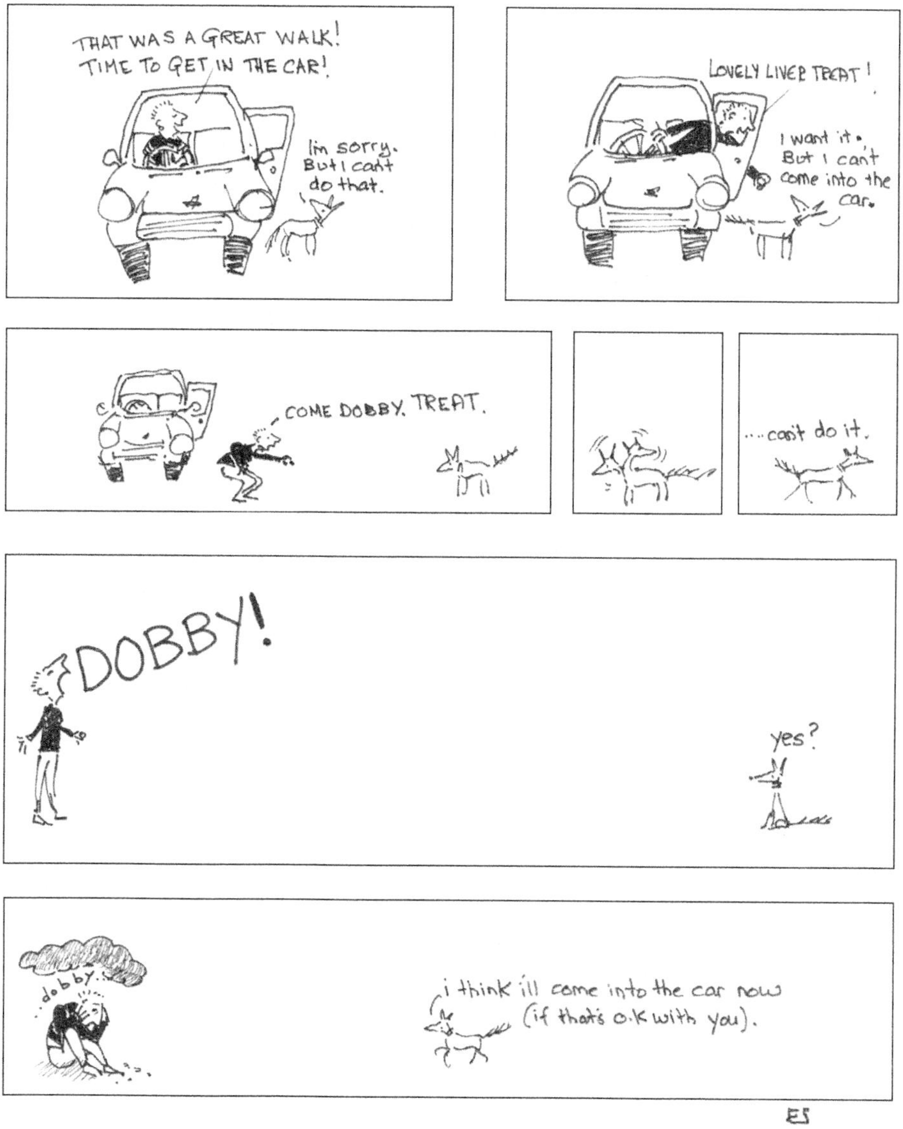
THAT WAS A GREAT WALK!
TIME TO GET IN THE CAR!
I'm sorry. But I can't do that.
LOVELY LIVER TREAT!
I want it. But I can't come into the car.
COME DOBBY. TREAT.
....can't do it.
DOBBY!
yes?
dobby...
i think i'll come into the car now (if that's o.k with you).
ES

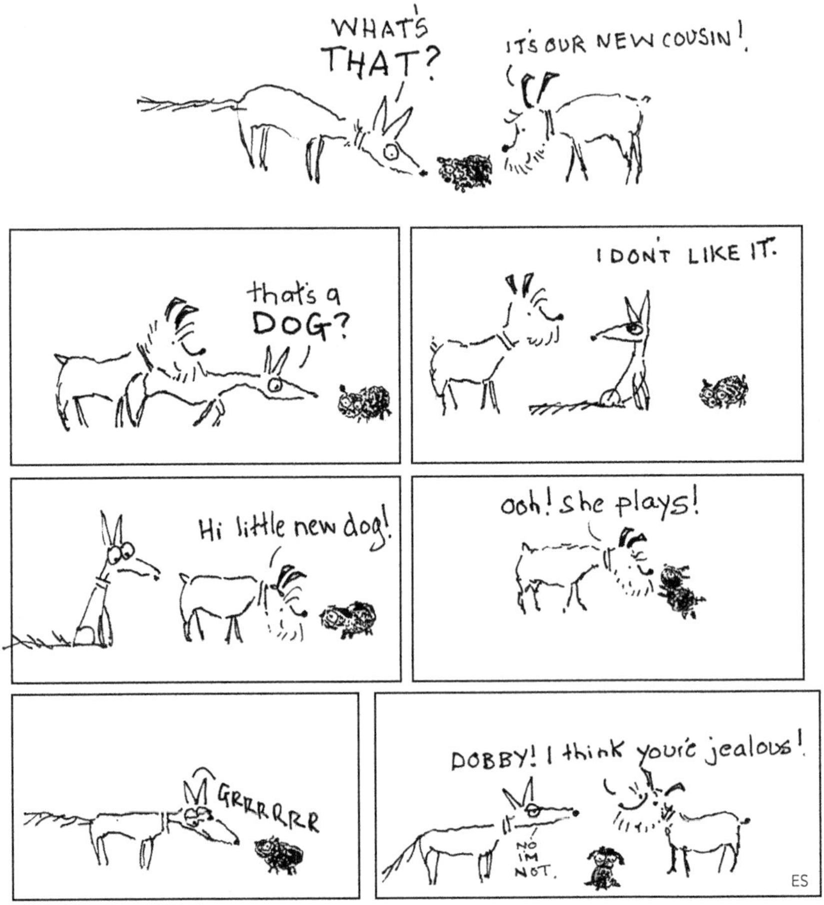
WHAT'S THAT?
IT'S OUR NEW COUSIN!
that's a DOG?
I DON'T LIKE IT.
Hi little new dog!
ooh! she plays!
GRRRRRR
DOBBY! I think you're jealous!
NO I'M NOT.
ES

what's it doing?
Chasing ants.
good grief.
dogs chase SQUIRRELS:
NOT ants.
I'M NOT CHASING
THAT!
ES

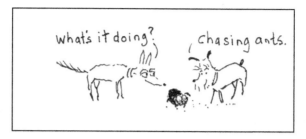

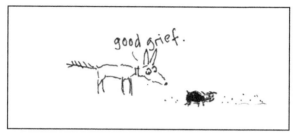

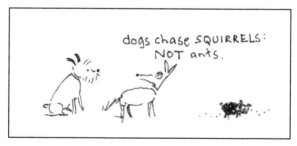

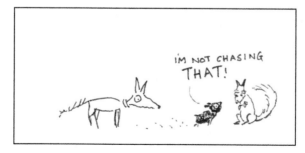

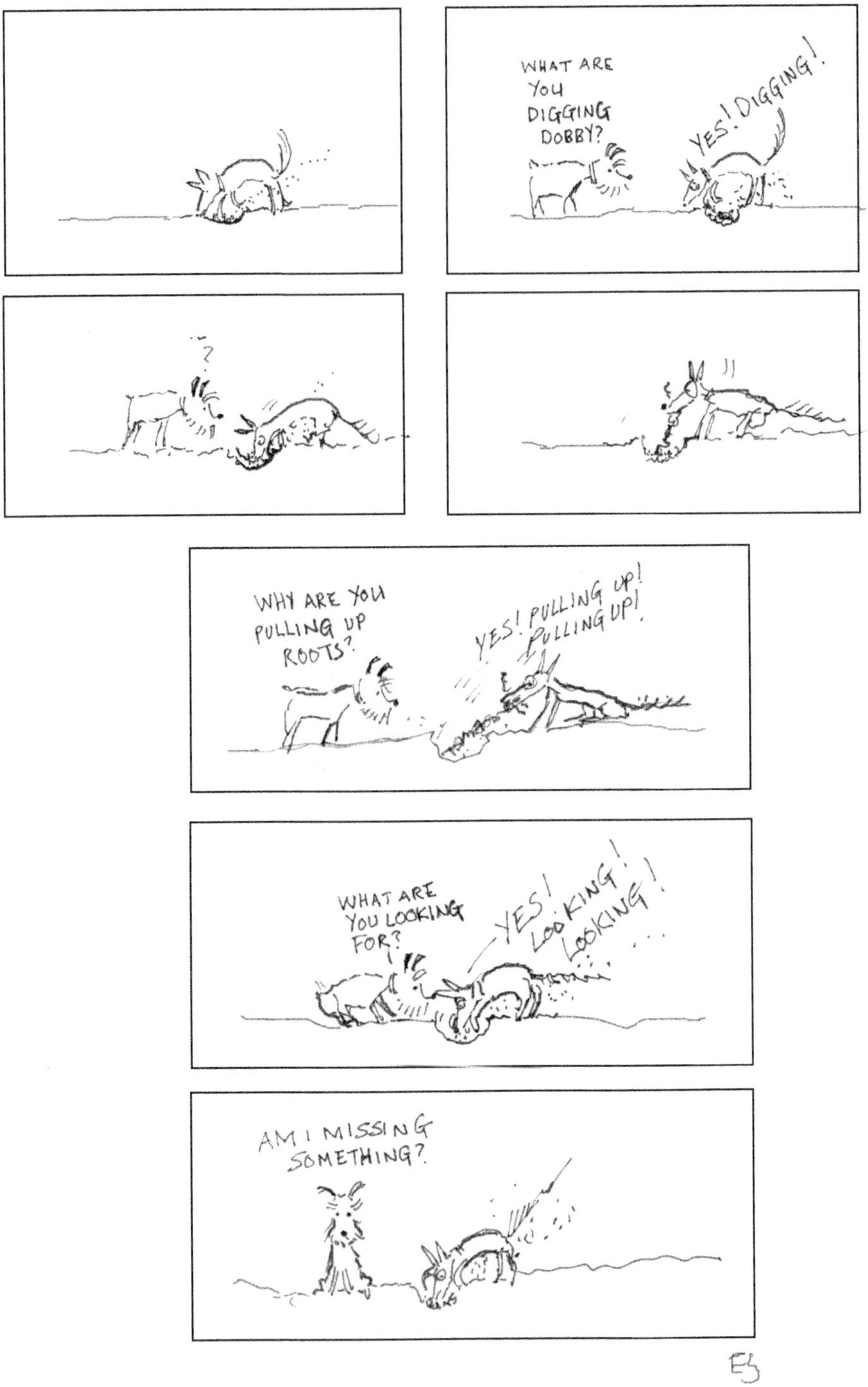
WHAT ARE YOU DIGGING DOBBY?
YES! DIGGING!
?
WHY ARE YOU PULLING UP ROOTS?
YES! PULLING UP! PULLING UP!
WHAT ARE YOU LOOKING FOR?
YES! LOOKING! LOOKING!
AM I MISSING SOMETHING?
ES

maybe we have something in common!
OH FOR GOODNESS SAKE! REALLY?
help!
T.S

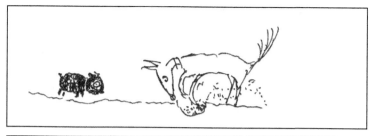

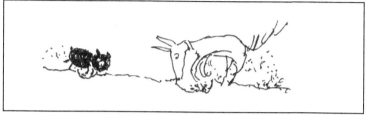

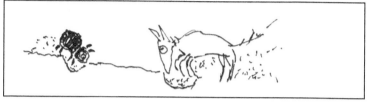

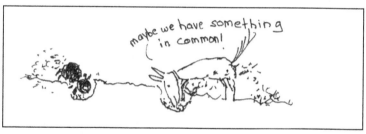

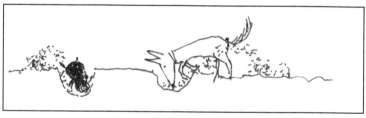

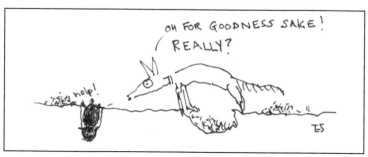

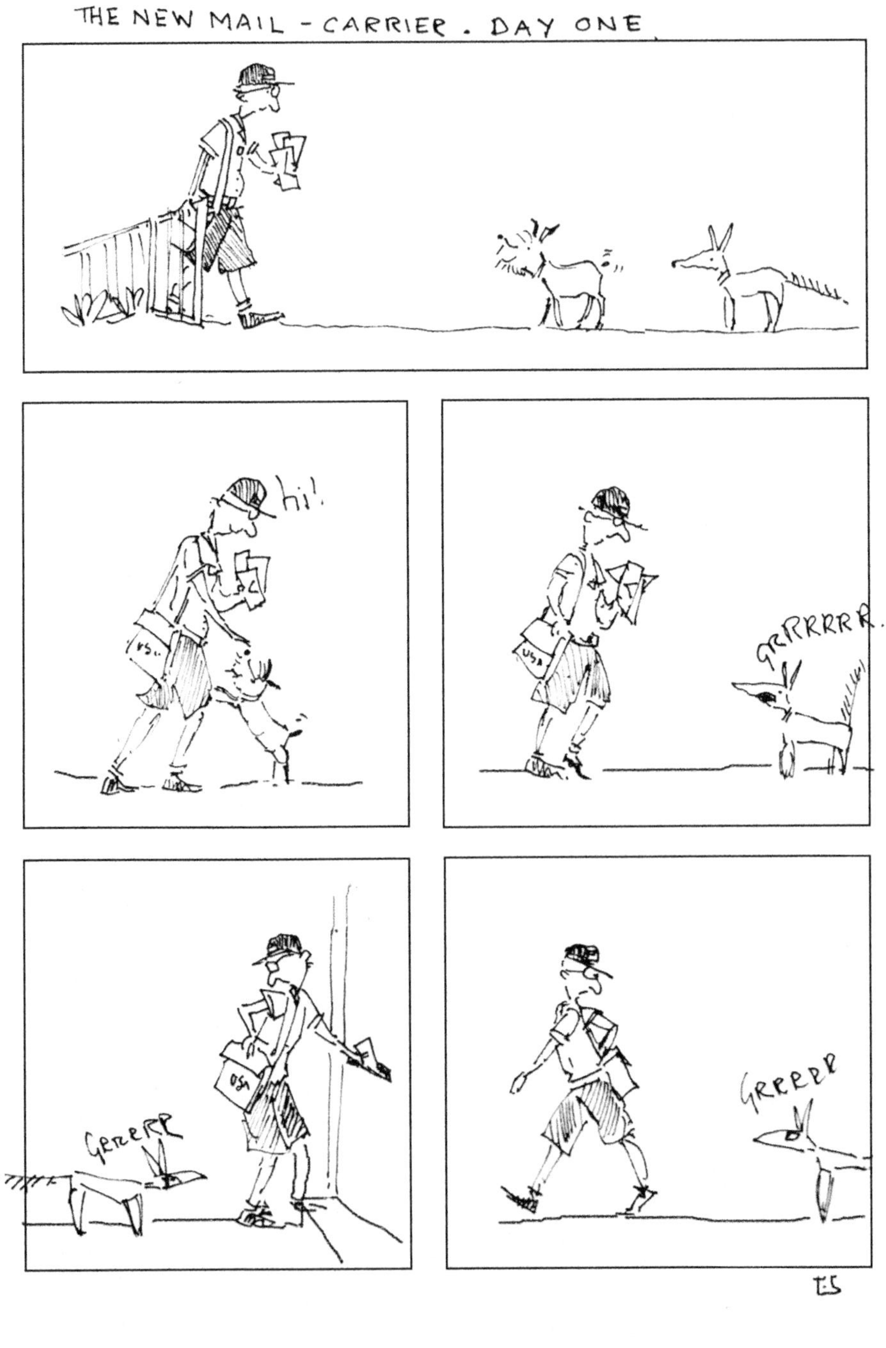
THE NEW MAIL - CARRIER . DAY ONE
hi!
GRRRRRR.
GRRRRR
GRRRRR
T.S

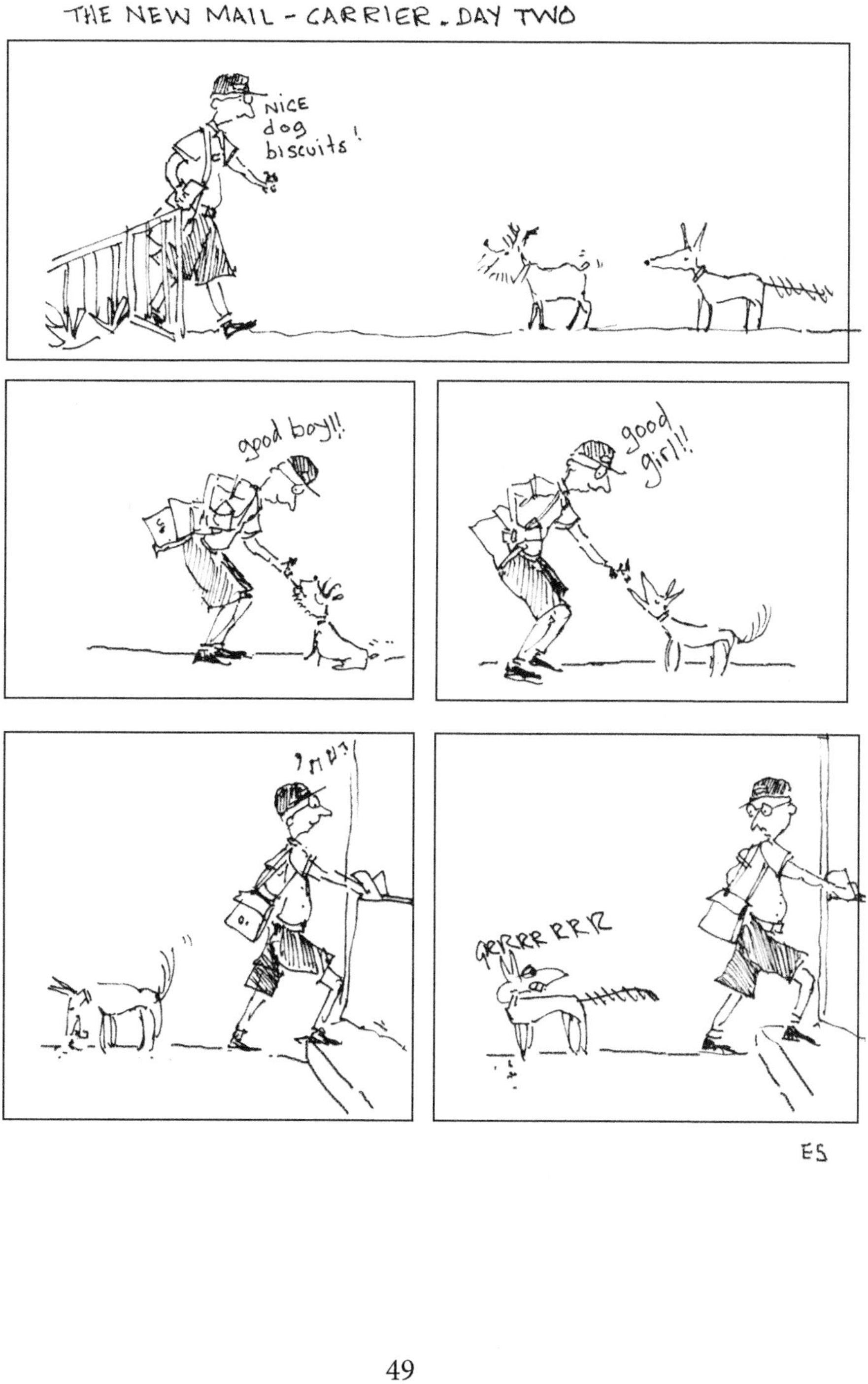
THE NEW MAIL - CARRIER - DAY TWO
NICE dog biscuits!
good boy!!
good girl!!
GRRRRRRR
ES

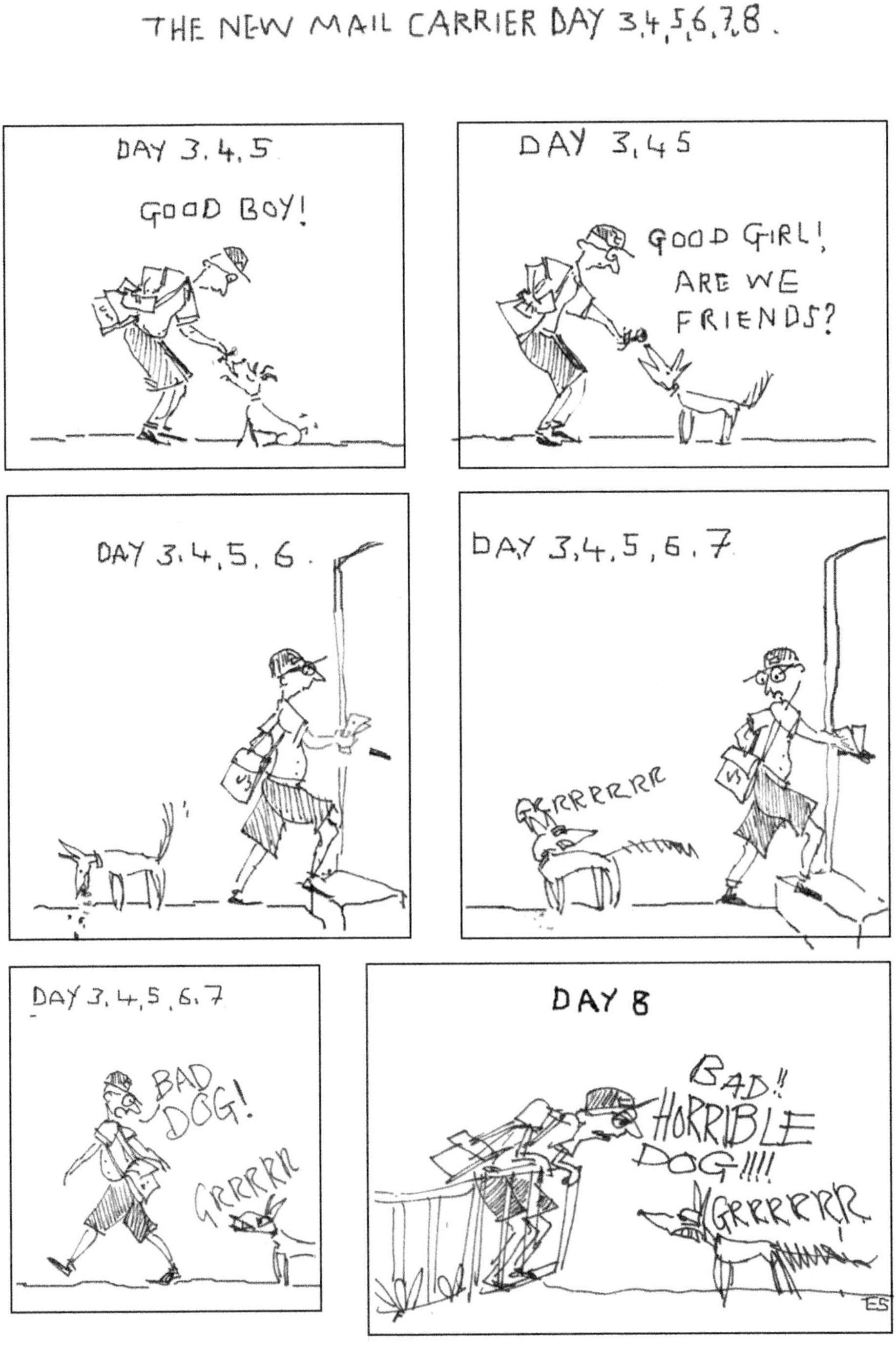
THE NEW MAIL CARRIER DAY 3,4,5,6,7,8.
DAY 3.4.5
GOOD BOY!
DAY 3,4 5
GOOD GIRL! ARE WE FRIENDS?
DAY 3.4,5. 6.
DAY 3,4.5,6.7
GRRRRRRR
DAY 3.4,5,6.7
BAD DOG!
GRRRRR
DAY 8
BAD!! HORRIBLE DOG!!!!
GRRRRRR
ES

HELP!!!

COME QUICKLY!!

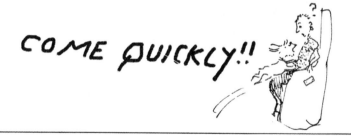

I THINK THE MAILMAN PUT SOMETHING BAD IN DOBBY'S BISCUIT!

ES

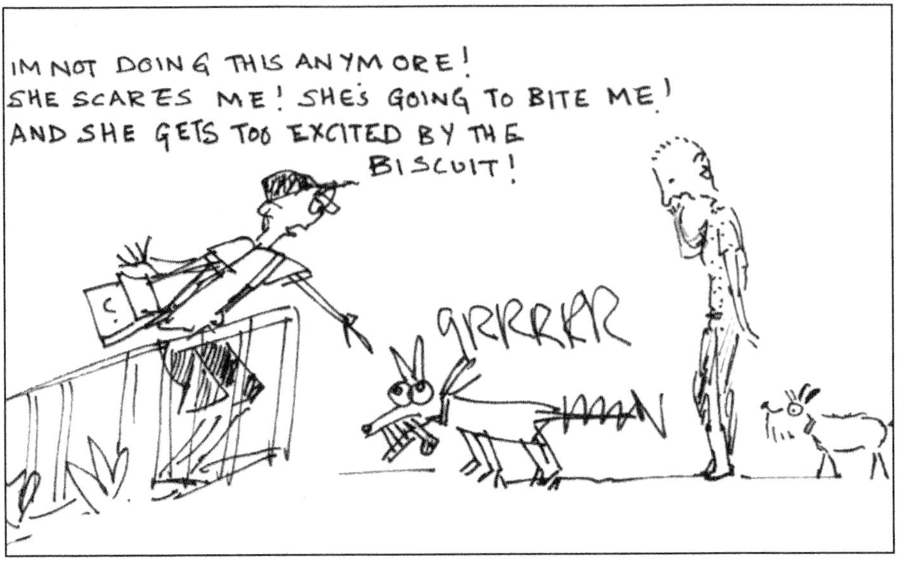
IM NOT DOING THIS ANYMORE!
SHE SCARES ME! SHE'S GOING TO BITE ME!
AND SHE GETS TOO EXCITED BY THE BISCUIT!
GRRRRRR

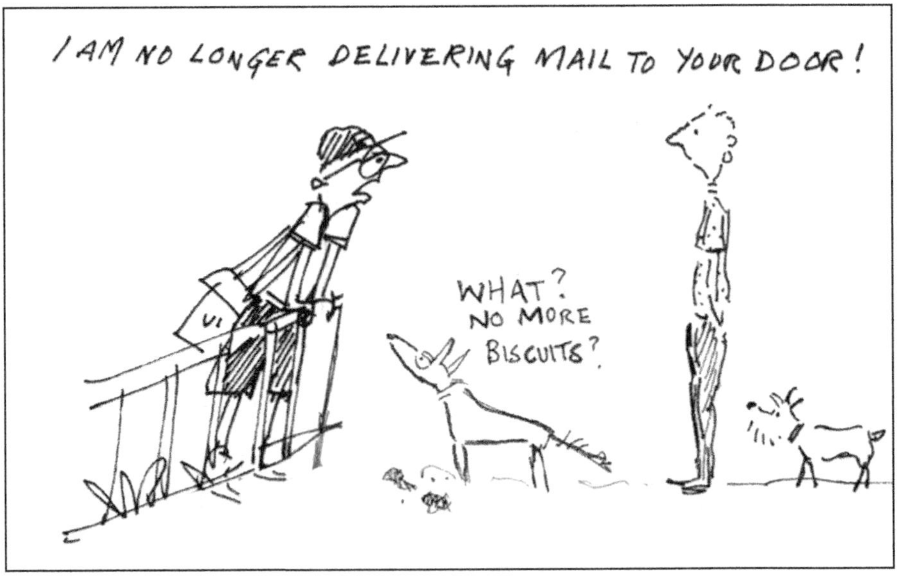
I AM NO LONGER DELIVERING MAIL TO YOUR DOOR!
WHAT? NO MORE BISCUITS?
ES

MAIL.
dobby this is all because of you.
THEY'RE PUTTING A GIANT BISCUIT JAR OUTSIDE OUR GATE!
WRONG.
you've become more of an optimist than i ever imagined

Elivia.

Other Books by Elivia Savadier

AUTHOR / ILLUSTRATOR

Roaring Brook Press
- NO Haircut Today!
- Time to get Dressed.
- WILL Sheila Share?

ILLUSTRATOR

Atheneum Books for Young Readers
- I Love Saturdays Y Domingos, with Alma Flor.

Scholastic
- The Uninvited Guest, with Nina Jaffe.
- The Mysterious Visitor, with Nina Jaffe.

Farrar, Straus and Giroux
- When you meet a Bear on Broadway, with Amy Hest.

Albums Circonflexe
- J'ai Perdu Ma Maman!, with Amy Hest.

Simon & Schuster Books for Young Readers
- Billy and the Bad Teacher, with Andrew Clements.

Little, Brown and Company
- Hotter than a Hot Dog, with Stephanie Calmenson.
- Grandma's Shoes, with Libby Hathorn.

Mondo
- A Bedtime Story, with Mem Fox.

Harper Festival
- Boo Hoo Boo-Boo, with Leslea Newman.

Harry N. Abrams. Inc.
- The Eight Nights of Hannukah, with Leslea Newman
- Jewish Holidays all Year Round, with Ilene Cooper.

Henry Holt and Company
- Las Nanas de Abuelita, with Nelly Palacio Jaramillo.
- I Swim an Ocean in my Sleep, with Norma Farber.

Houghton Mifflin Company
- Treasure Nap, with Juanita Havill.

Cambridge University Press
- Mama Mabena's Magic, with Diane Hofmeyer.

CPSIA information can be obtained
at www.ICGtesting.com
Printed in the USA
LVOW04s1330180416
484143LV00026B/585/P

9 780997 321906